Making Peace With Yourself

By Adrian Connock

The information provided in this book should not be treated as a substitute for professional medical advice; always consult a medical practitioner. Any use of information in this book is at the reader's discretion and risk. Neither the author nor the publisher can be held responsible for any loss, claim or damage arising out of the use, or misuse, of the suggestions made, the failure to take medical advice or for any material on third party websites.

ISBN: 9798484360277

Published by KDP Printing Press

Cover design by Adrian Connock

Original photography by Jeremy Vessey (Unsplash.com)

CONTENTS

Preface

This is a book about living in balance. It's a book that describes ways in which you can nurture your body, resolve imbalances in your mind and empower your life.

A collection of useful knowledge and lifestyle tips, compiled from many years of research, self-discovery and from working with numerous clients in a healing and psychological capacity. It addresses many of the central issues faced by people living in this modern age, whilst providing solutions, techniques and suggestions for staying healthy and enhancing well-being.

Every piece of advice in this book has been tested, experienced or validated by myself as being useful and effective. Although not every piece of advice will work for every individual, I hope that the breadth of resources will provide all readers with some worthwhile information they can apply to improving their life.

The contents of this book have been composed in a considered structure. Moving the reader through from the basics of health, to self-care techniques, to psychological advice, to recommendations about self-empowerment. It is not a manual filled with dogmatic instructions. Think of it more as a guidebook that you can take from what works for you. You may have glanced at the contents and thought that some of the chapters don't apply to you, but I do recommend reading them nonetheless. There is valuable knowledge presented that may be of use to you or could perhaps be useful for people you know.

The central themes in this book revolve around the process of self-reconciliation. Many of the health and psychological issues people face today are preventable, but are often perpetuated by self-criticism, self-depreciation and a lack of self-care. When a person makes peace with themselves, they accept themselves and care for themselves. They can then become strong, self-assured and move forward in life with ease. Making peace with yourself is the key to self-healing and self-empowerment.

As this is my first book to be published, I should probably say a few words about my experience. I've studied psychology, health and human potential topics for over twenty years, have a Bachelors in Psychology and Sociology, and have trained and worked as a counsellor. I have worked at holistic retreat centres around the world providing life coaching advice, therapeutic guidance and a range of healing services.

The information in this book has proven to be greatly valuable in my personal and professional life. I am happy to share it and sincerely hope it is beneficial for you.

CHAPTER ONE

Health Basics

Many people overlook the basic elements that are essential for living a healthy life. Therefore, in this opening chapter, I feel it is important to explain some of these elements. Firstly though, allow me to recount a short story about a friend of mine that illustrates this pervading oversight.

One of my old friends worked long hours in an office in London where he would usually eat lunch at his desk, and for much of the year would enter the building at dawn and exit the building at dusk. He developed fatigue, kidney problems and various other health concerns. He had been to see several doctors who had prescribed different medications, yet his health issues continued and the medications weren't making the symptoms any better.

One day, my friend visited the doctor's office, but on that day, there were no doctors available. However, a nurse from New Zealand, trained in naturopathy, happened to be on duty. She listened to my friend describe his symptoms and then asked him how much sunlight he was getting. My friend informed the nurse about his work in an office, the long hours, including the commuting, and that during the winter months he barely saw any daylight. She recommended he take some vitamin D supplements and get out in the sun when he could. Not long after following her advice, my friend was feeling much better.

I cannot recall any lessons at school providing the rudimentary instructions for maintaining health. Somehow, amongst all the hype about our scientific advancements, we have forgotten to teach people the basic steps for health. It wasn't until I was in my early twenties that I began to educate myself.

Clean water, sunlight, fresh air, nutritious food and regular exercise are the basic foundations for living a healthy life.

Clean water

Water is essential for bodily processes such as respiration, temperature regulation, digestion, metabolism and the elimination of waste. How much water to drink per day depends on your body size, your activity and the climate where you live — but on average a person should drink around 2 litres of clean water per day.

Sunlight

The life sustaining and vitamin D producing rays of the sun are essential for health and you should make an effort to get out into sunlight for some time every day. Even if the weather is cloudy, you will still receive some benefits from being outside in daylight. If you cannot get outside in daylight very often, then consider taking some high-quality vitamin D supplements.

Sunlight intensity varies depending on where you live on Earth and the time of year. For example, in some parts of Earth closer to the equator or at high altitudes, five minutes of sunlight will be the equivalent to one hour in a place further from the equator or lower in altitude. Use common sense when deciding how much sunlight to expose yourself to, and only use natural non-toxic sunscreen if absolutely required.

Fresh Air

Fresh oxygen is vital and it is recommended to spend at least half an hour outdoors everyday. If you live in an urban area, travel out to a more rural location at least twice a week — anywhere the air is fresh and not contaminated by pollution. A walk by the coast, a stroll in a forest or just an amble around a large park will rejuvenate you.

Nutrition

The subject of nutrition can get rather complicated and what works for one person may not work for another. There are thousands of nutrition related books, many of which recommend completely contradictory diets. From meat only diets to raw vegetable only diets. A lot of people get lost in the extremities. They may go overboard on juicing and don't realise they're not getting enough carbohydrates or they suddenly go vegan and don't have a clue how to get sufficient nutrition from their diet.

How people metabolise food widely varies due to physiological and genetic differences. There is no single diet that fits all and so you have to go with what works for you. Most nutritionists state that we all need specific amounts of fats, proteins, carbohydrates, trace minerals and vitamins. This is true to a certain extent, yet it is clear that humans are adaptable. Indeed, many people around the world have adapted to live without access to such a balanced diet. For example, there are tribes that live from a diet of corn beer and some seasonal root vegetables, and these people are found to be in good health.

The nutrient intake required for optimum health differs from individual to individual, and overtime, adaptations to different diets can occur. In general though, it is recommended to have a diet consisting of a variety of natural and non-processed foods. I have provided a list of foods in correspondence with their primary nutritional value in the Notes section, at the back of this book.

Hundreds of studies have revealed that a diet consisting of mostly processed and refined foods can be problematic. Processed and refined foods lose some of their original nutrient contents during the production process. And your body can then struggle to function optimally because these foods are missing nutrients that are required for proper metabolism. This often includes processed foods that are fortified with vitamins. Just because something is fortified with vitamins, doesn't necessarily mean the vitamins will be readily absorbed by your body. It is recommended to limit your intake of refined ingredients, such as white flour, white sugar and refined vegetable oils. And also processed foods, such as white bread, crisps, crackers, dried pasta, cakes and pizzas.

Many people eat more than they require and if you feel drained after you eat, then you should consider eating less. Often the reason for over-eating is because the body is craving some form of nutrient and will therefore keep the hunger bells ringing in the hope of receiving the nutrient it is deficient in. Sometimes, dehydration is also misinterpreted as hunger. If you eat a variety of natural foods then you will likely receive the nutrients you require and by monitoring how different foods make you feel, you can adjust your diet accordingly.

The three meals a day regime commonly espoused is not necessarily the right way for you. Some people benefit greatly from eating small amounts of food frequently, as opposed to three average sized meals per day. Experiment with eating different foods, different amounts, and at different times. Find what works best for you. For example, some people function much better by eating protein rich foods early in the day and carbohydrate rich foods in the evening.

What your ancestors ate can be a relevant factor to what diet will work best for you. It is also worth keeping in mind that your ancestors would have eaten mostly seasonal foods and many people find eating foods on a seasonal basis to be helpful for digestion. For example, if you live in the UK, you would eat apples only in the months they would naturally ripen on trees in the UK.

Eat in a peaceful setting when possible and take your time. In general, it is recommended to not eat whilst watching television, listening to radio or using a mobile device, as your digestion can be disrupted by the stimulus. It is not advisable to eat on the go or be engaged in an activity such as driving. Chewing slowly and thoroughly is beneficial and can aid digestion and the absorption of nutrients.

Many people benefit from movement, such as going for a walk or doing some stretching ten to twenty minutes after eating, and this movement can help with digestion. But it is recommended to rest and be inactive for about ten to twenty minutes after eating.

Keeping your body hydrated will assist in the digestive process, but don't drink any substantial amount of cold fluid shortly before, during or after eating — leave about fifteen minutes either side of eating. Warm beverages are best to have with food, and in moderation, will not interfere with digestive processes.

Incorporating some raw fruits and raw vegetables into your diet will provide you with enzymes more abundant with nutrients. Raw fruits and raw vegetables will also provide certain digestive enzymes that will help your body to break down other food types and allow nutrients to be absorbed. It is best to not overcook vegetables as excessive heat lessens the nutritional value. So, for example, you could quickly stir fry or steam vegetables. You can get a lot of nutrients absorbed quickly into your body by incorporating vegetable juices into your diet. Buying a juicer is a worthwhile investment that I strongly recommend.

Certain digestive enzymes are not available from food sources and are produced by the body to digest different types of foods. Some people are deficient in these digestive enzymes. A common example is lactase, which is a digestive enzyme used to break down dairy foods, and some people's bodies do not produce enough. If a person is deficient in certain digestive enzymes, the nutrients from the corresponding foods will not be sufficiently absorbed.

If you have any health issues thought to be caused by nutrient deficiency, you may be experiencing malabsorption. And you may benefit from making strategic changes to your diet in order to reacquire digestive enzymes. There are also supplements you can take if necessary. I have provided a relevant resource on the subject of digestive enzymes in the Notes section.

Looking after the balance of bacteria in your gut has

become recognised in recent years as being particularly important for health. If your diet consists of a lot of cooked foods, it will be beneficial to occasionally eat foods such as kefir, raw pickles, miso, sauerkraut or yogurt that contain beneficial bacteria and natural probiotics. You could also take a probiotic supplement such as acidophilus. Many nutritionists recommend to occasionally commit to a three to seven day 'Gut Reset' diet. This type of diet is primarily designed to reduce inflammation and reinstate a balance of healthy bacteria within your digestive system so it can function optimally. I have provided some links in the Notes section to easy to follow instructions for a Gut Reset diet.

Metabolism and digestion issues can also occur due to food intolerances. Gluten and dairy products are the most common culprits, yet in many cases, intolerances occur due to a lack of healthy bacteria and enzymes necessary to tolerate the food. If a person addresses these imbalances, they can often reintroduce the food in small doses without suffering any symptoms of intolerance. It has also been found that intolerances are sometimes not caused because of the food, but rather, because of toxic pesticides and fungicides. Therefore, intolerances can sometimes be resolved by simply switching to organic produce that usually contains significantly less toxins.

Food intolerances are sometimes being confused with allergies, but some people do have allergies to certain foods that can cause severe reactions. The advise given above is only applicable to those with mild symptoms of food intolerance, and should not be attempted to resolve any kind of severe allergy.

Eating more alkalising foods than acidic foods is recommended by many nutritionists for optimal health. There is some debate over the correct ratio, and everyone is slightly different, but approximately 75% alkalising food is usually suggested. One useful tip, is to squeeze half a lemon into water and drink this in the morning. Once digested, lemon turns highly alkaline in the body. So, if you have eaten a lot of acidic food the day before, you can counterbalance this quickly with lemon water. I have provided a list of alkalising foods in the Notes section at the back of this book.

Due to modern farming techniques, storage and transportation methods, there are less and less nutrients being found in foods, even in organic foods. Although it is best to source nutrition via food sources; high quality supplementation is worth investing in if you struggle to find the right balance of food in your area, or you need to address a deficiency that is causing health issues. People are commonly deficient in magnesium, zinc, iron, sulphur, omega-3, calcium, vitamin D or vitamin B12. In particular, if you are a strict vegetarian or vegan, you do have to make an effort to plan your diet and ensure you receive sufficient nutrition.

Nutrients are interdependent on each other in the body and therefore you don't want an excessive amount of one particular nutrient as that can cause deficiency in another. It is best to take supplements only when you feel like you really need them to complement your diet. If you do supplement, it is recommended to only take what you need, and then return to finding the nutrients from food sources, when possible. This way, your body doesn't become reliant on supplements.

If you are unsure whether you are deficient in certain nutrients, you can get a test done by a nutritionist or doctor to determine if you are deficient or not. But by looking at the list of foods provided at the back of this book in the Notes section, you can quite easily ascertain which foods to consume in order to receive a balance of nutrients.

CHAPTER TWO

Bypassing Toxicity

In this chapter, I review many of the common causes of bodily toxicity and provide tips for how to limit your exposure. I briefly refer to findings from studies that have linked exposure to toxicity with the formation of disease. However, you should keep in mind, there are always a multitude of factors involved with the formation of disease. So, for example, if a person consumes an excessive amount of the pesticide Glyphosate — this does not inevitably mean they will become ill.

Our bodies are very capable of dealing with toxins. And you should never become overly obsessed with trying to avoid toxicity, because in our modern world, it is simply not possible to fully avoid it. I've met some people who become stressed about having to occasionally eat non-organic foods, and this stress will impact their digestive processes and potentially cause issues. It's best to make some efforts to avoid toxicity, but to also trust that your body is well-equipped to cope. And there are ways to boost your body's natural detox processes, as I will discuss in the next chapter.

Food

Malnourishment is one of the leading causes of death around the world and vast numbers of people are suffering from illnesses as a result of malnutrition. Increasing rates of cancer, liver disease and heart disease, along with a multitude of other illnesses, are being linked to diets lacking in nutritional sustenance.

The increase of monocultured farming has led to a significant drop in nutrient levels in soil, and the nutrient content in many foods is subsequently decreasing. The widespread use of poorly regulated pesticides and other agrochemicals is being linked to a plethora of detrimental health effects ranging from depression, allergies, cancer, Autism, Parkinson's and infertility.

Genetically Modified (GM) foods are now being consumed in many countries around the world. Several studies have linked GM foods with cancer, liver and kidney damage, endocrine disruption and brain impairment. No long-term studies on the effects of GM foods on humans have been conducted. Many consumer products that are genetically modified are not being labelled as such. Whilst livestock animals and farmed fish are often being fed GM foods.

Large doses of refined sugars have been consumed by people for a number of generations and the effects of weakened immune systems, cardiovascular problems, obesity, hypertension, diabetes and psychological disorders have been well documented. Commonly consumed artificial additives and 'sweeteners' such as Aspartame, are also tied to an assortment of health issues such as premature births, cancer, memory loss, mood swings, seizures, fatigue and death.

The majority of supplements now contain very low concentrations of active vitamins and minerals, whilst a plethora of artificial ingredients are often included that actually increase toxicity in the body.

Here are some tips:

- Do your best to avoid genetically modified foods, artificial ingredients, heavily processed products, refined foods, irradiated food, and foods contaminated by plastic or metals. Do not worry if you cannot avoid these all of the time, as the human body is efficient at dealing with toxins.
- If you eat meat or dairy, then organic and free range is the best option as otherwise you will likely expose yourself to antibiotics or GM foods by proxy. Animals who lived in the sun and had a natural organic diet, will be higher in nutrients. This also applies to eggs produced by free range chickens who spend time in the sun.
- Grains that are soaked, sprouted or fermented will be easier to digest. Preparing grains through a slow fermentation process can provide higher nutrient levels. For example, sourdough bread is easier to digest and is high in B vitamins.
- Buy organic foods as often as possible. Organic foods will contain more nutrients, therefore, you'll need to eat less to feel satisfied, so it works out cheaper in the end.
- It is recommended to avoid non-organic gluten products as much as possible due to the high levels of toxic pesticides. A pesticide named Glyphosate is commonly used around the world, particularly on grain crops, and has been repeatedly linked to a number of diseases. Many non-organically produced foods are relatively uncontaminated

by pesticides. I have provided a link in the Notes section to a list of foods found to be the least contaminated.

- A rule that nutritionists often go by is, "If it's advertised on TV, don't eat it or drink it." It is best to avoid eating at the transnational corporate fast food chains. Also, you have to be aware that many companies will use the word 'natural' yet will still load the product with toxins — do not be fooled.

- Consume cold pressed oils or saturated animal fats. For example, you can use cold pressed olive oil to dress food. Coconut oil, butter or ghee to fry or bake. It is recommended to limit consumption of industrially produced 'vegetable oils' as many toxins are added during the manufacturing process.

- Be aware that some non-stick pans and aluminium pans can begin to leech toxic compounds over time. The health dangers of Teflon are clearly established. Well-produced iron pans without any non-stick coating are safer and will last much longer. You can buy iron pans that come 'pre-seasoned' and this provides a non-stick surface. Pans produced by Lodge, De Buyer or Solidteknics are recommended.

- Don't use microwave ovens as they can destroy nutritional vitality of food.

- Be highly prudent with any food or drink containing additional sugar. In particular, avoid the big-name corporate soda drinks that are heavily laden with refined white sugar. In moderation, use natural sweeteners such as coconut sugar, honey or maple syrup.

- For the most part, I suggest to avoid products with artificial ingredients such as colourings, 'flavourings' and preservatives. Usually, these are labelled as E numbers in the ingredient list.

- Sea salt is the most soluble type of salt for your body, and the less refined it is, the better. Celtic sea salt, also known as grey salt, is recommended for its high trace mineral content. It is best to avoid heavily processed and fortified table salts. Aluminium is often left over from manufacturing methods used to reduce clumping, whilst trace minerals such as magnesium are usually removed. Table salt will not be easily absorbed by your body.
- In terms of supplements, look for products that offer natural ingredients freeze dried and do not add toxic ingredients. Pukka Herbs, Veridian, Terra Nova and Thorne Research are noted for their good quality.
- Use toothpastes that are made from natural ingredients and do not have fluoride added.

Water

Tap water is usually not purified and is often contaminated with a host of toxins. Many water treatment companies routinely add chlorine, chloramine and fluoride. All of these chemicals are toxic to the body and have been linked to a range of diseases. A cocktail of microplastics, pharmaceuticals and illegal drugs are also increasingly being found in tap water, leading to the potential of many additional health effects.

Pure spring water naturally contains vital minerals such as magnesium and calcium. It will also be more oxygenated. To ensure you are drinking and absorbing clean water there are several options:

- Find a natural spring that you can go to and regularly fill up large containers. Get the water tested if you are unsure of the quality. This is easy to do, you just send a sample to a company who will test it for you.

- Buy a counter-top gravity water filter such as a Berkey or Osmio. You can fill them up with water from the tap and around 98% of impurities and toxins will be removed.

- Install a water filtration system such as a 'reverse osmosis system'. It is always best to buy a reverse osmosis system that also adds magnesium, calcium and other minerals to the water after it has been purified. You will have to get the filters replaced once or twice a year depending on which system you have and how much usage it gets. Prices for these systems and filter replacements are quite reasonable these days.

- If it is possible, hire a professional company to bore a well at your property.

- Add a pinch of unrefined sea salt to a one litre bottle of clean water and stir it in vigorously for a minute. The stirring motion will enhance the oxygen levels in the water, and the sea salt will add trace minerals.

- Buying bottled spring water is often a better option than drinking tap water. But do ensure it is spring water. If you buy the larger 5 litre bottles, they are usually made from thicker safer plastic.

- Avoid swimming pools that heavily chlorinate the water. There are non-toxic ways to purify water such as ultra-violet light. Search to see if there are non-toxic swimming options in your area. Wild swimming in clean rivers is recommended!

- Install a shower filter that is designed to remove toxins. These are quite inexpensive and very easy to fit yourself.

- Install a reverse osmosis system that purifies the water for your entire home and not just the kitchen tap.

Air

Air pollution is a major issue for much of humanity. Fumes from combustion engines, radon gas and industrial factories can contribute to a build-up of toxins in the body. Whilst volatile compounds released from man-made materials, fire proofing chemicals, common cosmetics and household cleaning products often contain a cocktail of toxic chemicals.

A wide variety of health issues ranging from respiratory problems, birth defects, fertility issues, depression and cancer have all been linked to air pollution.

To avoid and lessen detrimental effects of air pollution, it is recommended to:

- Open windows regularly to aerate rooms. If you cannot sufficiently ventilate because you live in an area with significant air pollution, you can buy some air filtration technologies. Blueair and Airfree are two manufacturers to consider purchasing from.
- There are many plants, such as Peace Lilies, Ficus, Chrysanthemum and Spider plants, that are known to clean volatile compounds from the air and can be utilised in your home. One in every room is recommended if you live in a polluted area.
- When driving in urban areas, keep your windows up and turn your fan system to recycle to avoid outside air pollution coming through. Glyphosate is being released into the air in many cities that are using biodiesel fuels.
- Avoid using synthetic perfumes, deodorants or air fresheners. There are non-toxic natural alternatives.
- Buy eco-friendly household cleaning products. Or you can easily make them yourself with natural ingredients by following simple instructions found online.

- If you are redecorating, it is best to use natural paints that do not contain toxic pollutants. Also, use glues and other construction and DIY products that have the best safety records.
- Ensure your home and work place are free from damp and condensation. Install trickle feed air vents and extractor fans in wet areas such as bathrooms. Ventilate naturally where possible. Eradicate any black mould or mildew.
- Do not purchase synthetic rugs or synthetic carpets for living spaces. Buy wool, cotton or sisal. Request that the carpet fitters use natural latex underlays and glues with a good safety record.
- If you have to wear a face mask for your job or because of health regulations, ensure you only wear natural fabric masks. The common blue face masks are made from synthetic materials and are being coated with toxic chemicals. Studies have shown a build-up of harmful bacteria occurs in all masks after extensive use. Change them every few hours and wash them regularly. Children should never wear face masks due to the dangers of preventing oxygen uptake to their developing brains.
- If you live close to industrial factories that cause air pollution then consider moving home. If you live near a nuclear power station or fracking site; move home as soon as possible.

Plastics and Petroleum

Exposure to oil based plastics and synthetic compounds, such as Bisphenol A and Bisphenol S, has been linked to infertility, cancer, endocrine system disruption, hormonal imbalances and brain impairment. Men living close to plastic producing factories have been documented to have significantly higher rates of infertility.

Hundreds of other synthetic 'plasticiser' chemicals, such as Parabens and Phthalates, are used in common cosmetics such as fake tans, perfumes, make-up, shampoos, hairsprays, deodorants and lotions. Many of these chemicals are linked to a wide range of health issues including infertility, diabetes, cancer, allergies and immune system damage.

Despite evidence of serious health impacts; millions of products implicated in hazardous exposure continue to be sold to consumers.

Here are some tips:

- Avoid using cosmetics or hygiene products that contain Parabens or Phthalates – there are natural and organic products that can be purchased as alternatives.
- Limit children's exposure to plastic products. In particular, avoid giving young children plastic dummies to suck on.
- Buy biodegradable plastic bags for rubbish and recycling needs. Use fabric bags at supermarkets and shops.
- When possible, avoid food wrapped in non-biodegradable plastic. Especially the thin plastic wrapping known as cling film. Buying organic veg boxes from farms who deliver to your door, usually means no plastic wrapping — and also much fresher food than from the supermarket.
- By ensuring a healthy balance of bacteria in your gut, you can limit the absorption of plastic toxins. Probiotics can reportedly be used to detox plastic from the body.

Metal Poisoning

Metal poisoning can result in behavioural and neurological disorders, amongst other problems. People can be exposed to metal poisoning via toxic metal dental fillings, contaminated food and drink, vaccinations, cosmetics, pharmaceuticals or air pollution.

Some dentists have moved away from using toxic metal fillings, yet some are still putting mercury fillings into people's mouths. These dental amalgams can outgas mercury into the mouth and sinuses, leading to high loads of toxicity.

Metals such as mercury and aluminium are still being added to some vaccines as preservatives, whilst mercury compounds are also being added to numerous products such as eye drops, nasal sprays and laxatives.

It is recommended to:

- Avoid dentists who still use mercury metal fillings. If you have to have an amalgam implant, then zirconium or titanium are much safer options.
- Avoid vaccines, especially those that contain aluminium or mercury compounds such as Thimerosal.
- Avoid using deodorants or any cosmetics with aluminium or other metals in.
- Do not use pharmaceutical products containing mercury compounds.
- It is best to avoid cooking with aluminium foil due to the possibility of metal poisoning.
- Research the content of metals being found in fish. For example, some types of Tuna should be considered off the menu due to the high concentrations of mercury often found.
- If possible, avoid spending long periods in areas impacted by high levels of air pollution. Ensure you have an efficient

air filtration system if living in an area with significant air pollution.

Pharmaceuticals

Pharmaceutical drugs have saved many lives and have certainly advanced modern medicine. Yet, they are also responsible for the deaths of tens of thousands of people every year. Safety regulations barely change and drug companies continue to push products onto the market despite trial indications of ill-effects.

Many commonly taken medications have side-effects. Statins can diminish cholesterol availability for cells and thus reduce the level of vitamins and nutrients being absorbed. Antibiotics can cause cellular damage and are linked with the rise of a number of diseases and syndromes due to the depletion of essential mitochondria, antioxidants, trace minerals and healthy gut bacteria.

- Take pharmaceutical drugs only when you think it is really necessary. If your ailment or illness is not serious or in urgent need of attention, then consider nutritional solutions and natural medicines as alternative treatments.
- Research pharmaceuticals before taking them, especially for contraindications with other drugs that you may already be taking. Doctors will often not check for contraindications before prescribing further medications.
- If you have any uncomfortable physical or mental symptoms that are unexplained, it is worth talking to your doctor about changing or stopping your medication to see if the symptoms clear up.
- If you do take antibiotics, consider implementing a Gut Reset diet afterwards to restore healthy balance to your

gut bacteria.

- Try not to ever get dependent on pharmaceuticals. Research alternatives and talk with your doctor and get a second or even a third opinion from different health professionals as necessary.

- At the time of writing, official databases reveal that the so called covid vaccines have been linked to over 40,000 deaths and six million injuries in the UK, EU and USA alone. The mRNA covid 'vaccines' are in fact gene therapy drugs. They are not effective at preventing infection or transmission. Illnesses being labelled as covid are very rarely severe, and there are numerous successful treatment protocols, such as the McCullough Protocol and the Zelenko Protocol.

Electromagnetic Radiation

Hundreds of distinguished and respected scientists have signed the '5G Appeal' and have pointed out evidence that electromagnetic radiation can cause a range of conditions such as:

- Neurological issues such as dizziness, headaches, confusion.
- Endocrine system problems and infertility.
- Oxidative stress and free radical damage.
- Cellular damage.
- Cardiac issues, strokes and seizures.

Yet, despite an abundance of scientific evidence for a wide range of serious health impacts, there has been no abatement of wireless technologies. Over the past two years, the new 5G wireless system has been rapidly installed around the world, exposing millions of people to increasing levels of electromagnetic radiation.

Compact Fluorescent Lightbulbs (CFL) can also cause health problems and have been found to emit carcinogenic chemicals including Phenol and Styrene. They are considered to be a risk to epileptic sufferers due to the intense flicker rate and high electromagnetic radiation emissions. Other health issues linked to these bulbs include skin damage, headaches, fatigue and cancer. However, health concerns are being side-lined by corporate producers, and EU health authorities have declared the much safer, easier to recycle, and mercury-free incandescent bulbs, to be phased out.

Lessen your exposure to electromagnetic radiation:

- Make phone calls using corded landline phones. You can easily forward your mobile calls to your landline phone whilst you are at home or in an office.
- Connect your computer to the internet via an ethernet cable then turn the wi-fi off on your router and device. You can purchase an inexpensive 'powerline' system and connect your computer via an ethernet cable from any power plug in the building, eliminating the need for lengthy cables. If your computer does not have an ethernet port, you can easily buy a cheap adapter to plug an ethernet cable in via a USB port.
- When you have to use your mobile phone, activate the loudspeaker. If it is not convenient to use the loudspeaker, do not push the phone against your head and keep calls as short as possible. Do not leave the wireless data stream activated all the time on your mobile devices, especially if they are in your pocket, disconnect the data or turn on airplane mode.
- Televisions, printers, cars and even appliances such as fridges are now coming with active wi-fi. You can usually

go through the settings and disable.

- Refuse to have any wireless Smart Meter installed by utility companies. If you already have one, insist that it is replaced with an old style meter.
- Do not sleep with any active wireless devices near to you.
- Do not use wireless headphones.
- You can change the network settings on your phone so that it will only connect with the 2G or 3G networks. Thus, avoiding the more powerful 4G and 5G.
- Do not use CFL light bulbs. Buy the halogen ones, Edison bulbs or if you can find them, the good old incandescent bulbs are best.
- Walk in nature, particularly on coast lines and in forests to restore vitality and balance to your bio-electric body. Earth yourself regularly by spending time barefoot on the earth.
- If you are sensitive to electromagnetic radiation, it is best to move out of cities and large towns to reduce your exposure.
- Be cautious if you are planning on purchasing an electric car as some have been found to emit dangerous levels of electromagnetic radiation.
- If your diet is mostly plant based, you may be more susceptible to electro-sensitivity due to high consumptions of copper. If you have symptoms such as fatigue or ringing ears, supplement with zinc and research the foods you are eating in order to moderate your copper consumption.
- To alleviate symptoms of electromagnetic radiation, some doctors recommend soaking in a bath in which you add a cup or two of Epsom salt.

Synthetic Materials

Toxic chemicals can be absorbed via skin contact with synthetic materials. Some materials are being made with chemicals such as Nonylphenols that are known endocrine disrupters. Clothes are also regularly being dyed with toxic compounds and are often covered in formaldehyde to prevent wrinkling. Synthetic 'anti-microbial' materials are now being widely sold and sometimes contain Triclosan and silver nanoparticles that have been associated with thyroid damage and hormonal disruption.

- When possible, purchase clothes that come from reputable companies and are made from natural materials. Cotton, bamboo, hemp or wool.
- The base clothing layers that come into the most contact with skin are more important. So, for example, a jacket made of synthetic materials will not be in contact with your skin much, as opposed to underwear, socks or a t-shirt. I recommend avoiding wearing polyester and other synthetic clothes as base layers, especially those that have synthetic 'anti-microbial' features.
- Buy bedding materials made from cotton, wool, kapok or bamboo.
- Natural latex mattresses are recommended and are normally not treated with toxic fire-retardants.
- Use eco-friendly and non-toxic cleaning products to wash your clothes and fabrics.

CHAPTER THREE

Detox Methods

After reading the previous chapter, you may be concerned about the toxins you've inevitably been exposed to in your life. However, your body goes through some form of detoxing process every day and is highly proficient at cleansing itself of toxins. As long as you do not allow your body to become overwhelmed with toxicity, it can manage very well. By making an effort to avoid toxins and by keeping your body hydrated, nourished and moving — whilst not being afraid of the inevitable toxicity you will encounter — your body will cope well.

That said, toxicity is presenting a problem for humanity and over 100,000 man-made compounds have been unleashed in our environment. Our body's innate detox processes have not had a chance to evolve ways to efficiently deal with all these new compounds, and can therefore become over-stretched.

Many people have unfortunately been inundated with

toxins throughout their lives. And the exponential rise in rates of physical and mental illnesses, such as cancer, dementia and depression is being linked to the accumulation of toxins in the body. Even less serious ailments such as fatigue, poor concentration, digestive issues and mood swings are being linked to biochemical imbalances caused by a build-up of toxins in the body.

Parasites and other infections caused by micro-organisms are also causing a range of health issues and are commonly undiagnosed. If you feel some toxicity or parasite infection may be affecting your health, there are many ways to amplify your body's natural healing and detoxification processes.

Fasting is one of the simplest. When a person abstains from eating solid food, it usually takes three days for faeces to stop eliminating and for the body to become more liquefied, and to start living off its own reserves. During this process, blockages are resolved, excess deposits are consumed, and toxins and parasites are processed more easily out of the body.

Fasting has been acknowledged in many studies as a way to initiate significant health benefits, including disease prevention. However, it should be noted, fasting is not recommended for pregnant or breast feeding women, children or teenagers, or for people with pre-existing medical conditions such as diabetes or high blood pressure. It is always advisable to speak with your doctor or a medical professional about dietary changes.

In general, it is not recommended to fast with only water. Many people are already deficient in nutrients, and fasting with only water can result in the body shedding some of its vital nutrients during the detox process.

Fasting with clean water and juice for four to ten days will provide your body with nourishment, whilst you also attain the health benefits of abstaining from eating solid food. If you do this type of juice fast at least once a year, you will protect your body from becoming overwhelmed by detrimental blockages or a build-up of toxins.

The following recipe provides an abundance of nutrients that will assist your body to cleanse and heal itself. There are other options that will work equally well, and you could consider purchasing a book on juicing. You will need to have a juicer for this method — a blender will not be suitable. So, you run the ingredients listed below through a juicer. Abstain from any food, drink plenty of clean water, and drink this juice for at least four days. The following quotas should provide you with enough juice for two days.

- 6 Lemons (rind removed)
- 12 Large Cucumbers
- 6 Romaine Lettuces
- 6 Beetroots (with stems and leaves)
- 6 Celery Sticks
- 1 Large Bag of Spinach (approximately 300 grams)
- 1.5cm Tumeric or Ginger

The above method may be all that you need for a sufficient detox regime. But there are more intensive detox protocols you could implement. So, you could fast with clean water and juice whilst also taking some triphala, coconut charcoal and bentonite clay. And by self-administering a coffee enema once a day during this detox, you can ensure bowel movements are regular and your lower digestive system is clear; allowing toxins and parasites to be flushed out efficiently. In the Notes section at the back of this book, you will find a link to a website where you can download free instructions for this type of detox method.

There are other detox protocols such as the 'liver flush' with apple juice, coffee enemas and Epsom salt or the 'master cleanse' with lemon juice, cayenne pepper and maple syrup. I have completed both of these detoxes and can attest to the health benefits, but these methods are often too intense for people and can cause uncomfortable symptoms such as nausea, headaches and anxiety. The previously mentioned detox protocol, that I have provided a link for the complete instructions, is a more effective overall detox method for removing toxins and parasites. And due to the use of 'binders' such as charcoal and clay, the chances of uncomfortable detox reactions are significantly reduced.

You should never detox half-heartedly. You will need to stick to at least four or five days of a detox method in order for the detox to be optimally effective. I have worked with many people during detox retreats, and the common causes of discomfort are invariably resolved by drinking more water. You have to drink many litres of water each day during a detox to assist your body in flushing out toxins and/or parasites.

If you are in good health, then it is perhaps not necessary for you to complete a detox program. But many people will find detoxing to be highly beneficial.

The health benefits most commonly experienced after a detox are:

- Increased energy
- Better digestion
- Clearer skin and reduction of bodily odour
- Restorative sleep
- More creativity

- Longer concentration
- Improved memory
- Strengthened immune system
- Increased calmness

However, if a person then returns to eating a diet low in nutrients, not drinking enough clean water and doing hardly any physical exercise, the health benefits of the detox will be short lived.

By taking steps each day towards avoiding toxins and by keeping your body sufficiently hydrated, nourished and moving — you will naturally enhance your health and optimise your body's detoxing capabilities.

Here are some tips for maintaining a gentle, but consistent detox protocol in your life:

- Maintain hydration. Drink at least two litres of water each day. Preferably filtered or spring water.
- Certain foods are more abundant in compounds that can assist the body to detox and it is recommended that some of these foods are in your diet on a regular basis. I have provided a list in the Notes section at the end of this book.
- You can try intermittent fasting. So, you only eat during a six to eight hour window per day. This allows your body to operate more from fat rather than sugar. And this change in metabolism also allows your body to detox more easily. Intermittent fasting may not be suitable for pregnant or breast feeding women, children or teenagers, or for people with pre-existing medical conditions such as diabetes or high blood pressure.
- Sweating through exercise, saunas or steam rooms is an effective and simple way to purge toxins out via the skin. Shower with cold water for at least a minute after any

significant sweating to wash away toxins most efficiently.

- Maintain good hygiene and wash everyday. Your body naturally detoxes via your skin even if you are not sweating profusely.
- The processes known as 'oil pulling' and 'tongue scraping' can assist your body in detoxing and are easy to implement into your lifestyle.
- Regularly practice deep breathing — preferably in a place where there is clean air. If your body is highly oxygenated, your natural abilities to detox will be boosted.
- Maintain a healthy microbiome. Healthy gut flora can prevent the absorption of toxins. You can initiate a 'Gut Reset' by following an easy to implement diet for three to seven days.
- Stress and worry can affect your digestive system and your immune system. It is recommended as part of maintaining your health, to address negative emotions, relationships and situations that may be toxic and causing you harm. I will talk more about this in later chapters.
- For two months after any detox where you think you have cleared parasites. Take two capsules of pure oregano oil, and four coconut charcoal capsules every four days. Stay on a strict low sugar diet consisting of small sized meals for at least six weeks. These tips can help to clear any remnants of a parasite infection. You should consult with a medical professional or naturopath about more specific advice.

Boosting Your Immune System

By boosting your immune system, you will also boost your body's ability to detox. If you are prone to illness and infection, then definitely consider boosting your immune system using the following method.

For three consecutive days:

- Initiate a 'Gut Reset' diet for 3 days (links to diet details provided in Notes section).
- Don't eat anything high in sugar, including high fructose fruits such as bananas.
- Take 2.5 grams of buffered vitamin C powder twice a day. In between meals is recommended.
- Supplement with 60 mg of zinc once a day with food.
- Supplement with 200 mcg of selenium once a day with food.
- Spend at least 15 minutes in direct sunlight each day. If this is not possible, supplement with 50 mcg of vitamin D3 each day.
- Exercise for at least 15 minutes each day — preferably outside. If you have sweated profusely, take a shower with cold water for at least 1 minute afterwards.
- Drink plenty of clean water.
- Once a day, practice at least one of the relaxation techniques I provide in the later chapter Relaxation Techniques. Stress inhibits your immune system and also inhibits your body's abilities to detox. By managing your stress levels and dearousing your nervous system, your immune system will function more efficiently.

*Supplement qualities vary. The supplement measurements stated above are based on three Terra Nova products: Selenium, Zinc and Vitamin D3. Also, Thorne Research Buffered Vitamin C Powder. Unless you have consulted with a medical professional or qualified nutritionist who provides specific instructions; check the label and take the recommended dose of any supplement you purchase.

Testing For Toxicity

If you suspect your health is being affected by toxicity or parasites, there are various tests you can have that are carried out by health professionals. It can be helpful to know what you are dealing with because specific treatment methods and detox protocols can then be applied.

These tests are sometimes inaccurate and so it is worth considering getting two or more types of test if you want to be sure of a result. But you do also have to remember, many of the tests carried out by doctors and nutritionists, do not test for thousands of chemical compounds and toxic substances that you could have been exposed to.

Urine tests are usually more accurate than hair sample tests or blood tests if you are trying to ascertain whether you are suffering from toxic metal poisoning. For severe cases of metal poisoning, there are professional Chelation services available in some countries.

CHAPTER FOUR

Movement, Exercise & Bodywork

The benefits of regular exercise are numerous. Just thirty minutes of exercise three times a week is all that is required as a base minimum. Hundreds of studies have shown a wide range of positive health effects. Some highlights include:

- Improved heart health and blood pressure.
- Improved cholesterol levels.
- Improved regulation of hormones.
- Improved digestion.
- Increase in testosterone for men.
- Burn off stress hormones such as cortisol.
- Neurogenesis — the growth of new nerve cells and new synapses, leading to increased capacity of the brain.
- Increased endorphins and neurotransmitters such as serotonin, leading to elevated mood.
- Helps to prevent and alleviate depression, anxiety, hyperactivity and neurodegenerative disorders such as

dementia.
- Increased life span.
- Cancer prevention.
- Strengthening of bones.
- Improved regulation of blood sugar and insulin levels, leading to reduced risk of type 2 diabetes.

Balance

Throughout evolution our ancestors were physically active much of the time — farming, foraging, collecting water, hunting, making clothes and building shelters. Tasks were varied and required a range of physical movement and exertion. There simply wasn't a lot of time to sit down due to the many day to day chores related to survival and prosperity.

Yet, in modern times, people often spend much of their life sat down, either at work at a desk, driving a car or at home on a sofa. In terms of food, we now go to supermarkets and push around a trolley, in terms of water we turn on a tap, in terms of heat we press a button. There are very few physical activities directly carried out for our survival needs anymore. Most modern jobs do not exert a person physically, and even the jobs that require physical work, often only require a limited range of movement.

When one looks at common exercise practices in gyms, it is clear that a recommended program replicates much of what a person would have been doing if they were living from the land. Lifting, pulling, pushing, squatting, carrying, running, climbing etc. Our bodies evolved to be as they are by being used in a multitude of ways, and that is what we have inherited though evolution.

We need to move and exert our bodies regularly in a wide range of ways to maintain physical agility and balance. Are you moving your body in a range of motions? Are you exerting yourself through sustained movement? And are you getting a balance, whereby you move and exercise enough to maintain the totality of your body?

Over the course of two weeks, take notes as to what movement and exercise you do regularly. Would you benefit from making some changes? For example, if you are active cycling and walking, but don't exert your upper body in any significant ways, it will be beneficial to do some upper body stretching and strengthening exercises. Perhaps some core strengthening exercises such as those found in Pilates will also be helpful.

There are many home workout videos available for free on Youtube. You can find an instructor by searching for phrases such as 'full body workout' or 'full body warm up'. Some of these videos are only ten or fifteen minutes long and are ideal to implement as a daily exercise practice.

If you are not sure what is best for you, consulting with a personal trainer can help to reveal what parts of your body are out of balance. You can either choose to follow their program at the gym or take their advice and find ways to adjust your lifestyle and bring balance to your body.

The Mind Body Connection

One of the major issues for people in modern societies is stress. Stress causes tension in the body, and if the stress continues, tension can become chronic and leave a person vulnerable to physical and mental imbalance.

Many psychologists and psychotherapists are now

combining therapy sessions with exercise programs. Some are also recommending movement and exercise regimes to their clients, as part of treatment protocols for depression, anxiety and other imbalances.

It is an interesting practice, to become consciously aware of how you feel in your body, and to realise how different emotions and sensations affect your body. Where do you feel grief? Where do you feel shame? Where do you feel joy? Where do you feel happiness? Where do you feel stress? And what do you feel?

What you will likely realise, is there is a connection between your emotional states and the sensations and feelings you experience in your body. Many people don't stop to notice this. For example, if a person feels afraid, they will often experience a tightening sensation in their stomach area. If they feel joy, they will often feel a loosening and expansive sensation in their chest area.

More and more research is confirming that negative emotions are often contributing factors to many ailments and illnesses. This is partly because certain emotions result in tension being held in certain areas of the body. And if this tension continues for long periods, it can lead to detrimental health impacts.

The opposite is true for positive emotions. And positive life experiences have been shown to have beneficial physiological health effects. This is largely due to their calming and easing effects on the body and mind. In particular, good friendships, loving relationships and positive feelings generated from fulfilling tasks; have all been found to have beneficial physical and psychological effects.

By releasing negative emotions, you can relieve tension in your body. There are many ways to achieve this. But you should never overlook the simplicity of movement and exercise for relieving both physical tension and mental stress.

Movement and exercise practices that encompass a body and mind approach can be particularly effective at relieving tension and stress, due to facilitating a harmony and equilibrium between the body and mind. Yoga, Chi Gong and Tai Chi are prime examples, whereby movement and exercise are combined with breath-work, meditation and lifestyle changes that further engender calmness. These practices can also help develop the connection between body and mind, and can assist in releasing stress and tension that may be stored simultaneously in the body and mind.

It is helpful to attend classes, get a DVD or sign up for online classes, but once you've got the basics you can create your own format and discipline. These ancient practices are very much rooted in the concept of following what your body intuitively wants to do, and they encourage people to develop a mental trust in the innate wisdom of their body. You may have found yourself at times doing certain stretching movements spontaneously. The body tends to know what it needs. Learn to trust your body's own wisdom and then move and exercise in ways that feel most needed and beneficial for you.

Dance is a great way to move and exercise in spontaneous ways. Dance can also serve to release stored emotions. You could sign up for dance classes or just freestyle dance in your living room. Shaking parts of your body is also an effective way to release tension and stress, and these methods are often incorporated into Yoga and Chi Gong practices.

If you are sitting for much of the day, ensure you have a healthy posture and that your body is correctly supported. Implementing 'exercise snacks' can serve to release physical and mental tension. So, after every hour of sitting, you would get up and exercise for three minutes. Simple squats, a jog on the spot, some stretching or a brief walk will be beneficial for body and mind.

There are many bodywork modalities that can help to resolve issues caused by poor posture, injury or stress. Massage, fascia massage, Shiatsu, Rolfing, chiropractic treatments, cranial-sacral therapy and physiotherapy are some examples.

You can also further your understanding of your body by learning about acupressure points and the lymph node system. You can then learn how to self-massage, or apply simple pressure or tapping techniques to relieve yourself of tension. I have provided a couple of links in the Notes section as a starting point.

CHAPTER FIVE

Relaxation Techniques

It is natural to sometimes feel stressed, and a certain amount of stress can be motivational to take positive action. However, in today's modern societies, an increasing amount of health problems are being linked to chronic stress.

Stress can impact every aspect of your life — your body, mind and relationships. In particular, stress can impact the enteric nervous system, a system of neurons in the gut. When the enteric nervous system is consistently impacted by stress, illnesses such as ulcers, irritable bowel syndrome or Crohn's disease can develop.

Adrenal fatigue is another common issue that can occur due to sustained stress levels. This is caused by excess production of hormones, such as cortisol. Stress can also have a substantial impact on the neurons in the heart, and can disrupt the communication between the heart and the brain.

If you think you have difficulty recognising when you are

stressed, you can look to your body and to your thoughts, words and actions for signals. Stress is noticeable in a multitude of ways. Through the language we use, the sounds we make, our body posture, and physical manifestations such as clenching of muscles, a high pulse rate, stomach pain, sweaty palms, grinding of teeth, tight lips or frowning. Tension in your body is always a sign of unease and stress.

People are often unequipped to cope with stress, yet there are simple relaxation techniques that can be practiced to prevent and alleviate stress. I will outline some easy to learn methods for inducing relaxation in this chapter.

Many positive things can happen when you relax. You can release stress and tension, and also process and let go of emotions. Trust that your body and mind have an intelligence and a natural propensity to heal, in particular, when you are relaxed.

Practicing relaxation techniques regularly has been shown to:

- Reduce cortisol levels.
- Improve immune system functioning.
- Improve digestion.
- Improve heart and vascular health.
- Reduce symptoms of anxiety.
- Reduce pain.
- Prevent hyperventilation and panic.
- Increase a sense of peace and well-being.
- Increase creativity.
- Lead to more restorative sleep.

Breathing Techniques for Relaxation

When people become stressed they invariably breathe faster and shallower. If you ever start to feel tense or stressed, it is good practice to notice how you are breathing.

To calm yourself, focus your attention on your breathing, and allow yourself to gradually change the rhythm so that you are breathing slower and deeper. Go at your own pace and very gradually slow and deepen your breathing rhythm. Take your time and don't try to rush.

By breathing more slowly and deeply you activate the relaxation response in your body. Both your body and mind will then become calmer. You simply cannot be relaxed and stressed at the same time, one counterbalances the other. Slow and deep breathing is the most effective way to induce relaxation.

Many people recommend to practice the following breathing techniques through the nose only, and this can oxygenate the brain and calm the mind quicker, however, I have found that it doesn't matter a great deal. It is best to practice in the way that you feel most comfortable with. I often breathe in through my nose and out through my mouth, but you can experiment and find what works best for you.

Breathing Method 1:

• Sit comfortably in a chair where your back is supported or lay down in a comfortable position on your back.
• Bring your awareness to your breathing, monitor your in-breath and your out-breath for a minute or so.
• Then gently begin to slow your breathing rhythm, inhaling

for slightly longer and more deeply — and also exhaling for slightly longer. At a pace that is comfortable for you, continue to further slow your breathing so that you are taking long deep breaths in and out. Your abdomen will rise up as you breathe in deeply to use the full extent of your lung capacity.

- As you breathe slowly and deeply you will naturally become more deeply relaxed. Notice any tension loosening and being released from your body as you continue to further relax.
- If any thoughts or emotions arise, agree to think about them later, and say to yourself, "Now is not the time to worry, this is the time for me to relax." Then return your focus to the rhythm of your breathing.
- You can enhance this exercise by saying in your mind the word, *Relax*, each time you exhale.
- Practice this simple breathing exercise for between five and twenty minutes.

Breathing Method 2:

- This method can be done anywhere at any time and you simply focus on breathing out for longer than breathing in.
- Some people like to count in their mind. 3 seconds breathing in then 5 seconds breathing out. And in your own time, gradually increase to 7 seconds breathing in and 11 seconds breathing out.
- Practice this exercise for five to ten minutes if you feel stressed. This is the most effective method for overcoming anxiety or panic as you will offset hyperventilation.

Breathing Method 3:

- Close your eyes and slow your breathing rhythm as described in Method 1.

- When you feel more relaxed, take a deep breath in and hold your breath for around 3 seconds and on the exhale, breathe out of your mouth slowly so that you make a shushing sound as you exhale. So, you open your mouth just a little to slowly exhale. Keep breathing out slowly and add a little force at the end of the exhale to expel every last molecule. Then breathe in again and hold for 3 seconds, and repeat the exhale slowly process.

- Repeat this process five to ten times. As you become more relaxed you will feel any tension leaving your body with every exhale.

- If holding your breath for 3 seconds is not comfortable, you can hold for less.

The following techniques are best practiced in a quiet environment where you will not be distracted or interrupted. It is recommended to turn off televisions, radios, phones and internet enabled devices. Inform people in your home as necessary, so you are not disturbed unless there is something that cannot wait.

Playing some relaxing music whilst practicing these techniques can be very beneficial and can also help you to keep track of time without having to set an alarm. Minimal ambient music without lyrics is usually most suitable.

I recommend to practice the following techniques laying down on your back, whilst resting your arms at your sides and not crossing your legs. Find a comfortable position and for example, you may want to support your head, place a pillow under your knees, remove your shoes, wear loose fitting clothes and ensure you are warm enough.

Body Scan Relaxation — Method 1:

- Lay down on your back in a comfortable position.
- Close your eyes and gradually slow and deepen your breathing rhythm.
- Bring your awareness to your body and in your mind's eye, scan your body slowly from your toes to your head, consciously sensing each part of your body as you slowly scan up your body.
- Then scan your awareness back down your body and become aware of your feet.
- Make a conscious effort to relax your feet, so that you sense and feel your feet relax. You may find you wiggle or stretch them a little in the process, and when you feel they have relaxed, you are ready to move your awareness up to the next area of your body.
- Go through this process with every major part of your body moving upwards from your feet. I usually bring awareness and relaxation in this order:
  - Feet, ankles, calves, thighs, buttocks
  - Lower back, stomach, chest
  - Hands, forearms, biceps
  - Shoulders, neck, forehead, face, jaw, eyes
- As you bring your awareness to each part of your body, sense it for a few moments and then consciously relax it. So, you sense and feel the area of your body relaxing. You will likely find yourself moving a little at times to get more comfortable as you further relax. It is a good thing to follow

any feelings you have, for example, to shrug your shoulders, to stretch an arm out for a moment or to open wide your jaw for a moment. Just go with what your body wants to do in order to relieve tension and get more comfortable.

• After you have completed scanning and relaxing each part of your body, you can either choose to repeat the process; going back to your feet and coming up your body again whilst consciously relaxing each part of your body, or you can simply rest in the relaxation for as long as you want.

Body Scan Relaxation — Method 2:

This is the same method as above but you will be actively tensing and contracting each area of your body before letting go and relaxing. When you purposefully tense your muscles and then release the tension, they will always be more relaxed than they were previously.

• Lay down on your back in a comfortable position.
• Close your eyes and gradually slow and deepen your breathing rhythm.
• Bring your awareness to your body and in your mind's eye, scan your body slowly from your toes to your head, consciously sensing each part of your body as you slowly scan up your body.
• Then bring your awareness down to your feet and actively tense and contract the muscles there. So, most people would clench their toes and stretch their feet outwards. Then after five to ten seconds release the contraction and relax your feet.
• Go through this process with every major part of your body moving upwards from your feet.

- I usually bring awareness, muscle contraction and relaxation in this order:
    - Feet, calves, thighs, buttocks
    - Lower back, stomach, chest
    - Hands, forearms, biceps
    - Shoulders, forehead, jaw, eyes
- As you bring awareness to each part of your body, sense it for a few moments and then contract the relevant muscles and hold the resulting tension for five to ten seconds, then release the contraction and relax.
- After you have completed this for each part of your body, you can repeat the process one more time or simply rest in the relaxation for as long as you want.

It can be helpful to practice these body scan relaxation techniques by listening to a recording of a person guiding you through the process. There are many versions available and by searching online for 'body scan meditation' or 'progressive body scan relaxation audio' you will be able to find one to listen to for free or to purchase. You can also check my website.

The following techniques involve visualisation and imagination. Visualisation is focusing your mind to produce mental imagery. If you have any difficulty with visualising — practice by closing your eyes and creating a mental image of anything you are familiar with. So, your best friend's face, your pet's face, your bedroom, your front door, your car, your feet on a beach or your hands placed on a table. The vast majority of people can visualise very well, yet have rarely practiced. Don't worry if you can't hold the image for very long.

What you can do next is practice visualising short clips of moving imagery in your mind — short movie clips you could say. So, in your mind, watch your best friend's face as they smile and laugh, or watch your pet play with one of their toys, or see yourself opening your front door, driving your car, swimming in the sea etc.

You can also practice incorporating other sensations such as smells, touch, taste and sound. For example, visualise yourself walking along a beach and notice the sound of the waves, the fresh scent of the sea air, the touch of the sand on your feet and the slight taste of salt in your mouth as a gentle breeze blows past you.

The Healing Colour Visualisation — Method:

- Lay down on your back and get comfortable ensuring you are warm enough.
- Close your eyes and gradually slow and deepen your breathing rhythm.
- Begin to visualise your body being bathed in a soothing colour. Perhaps purple will work for you or gold, magenta, turquoise or deep blue — find a colour that feels most soothing.
- For a few minutes, visualise your body being surrounded by your soothing colour.
- Allow yourself to notice any tension in your body and bring your awareness to these areas one at a time and visualise your soothing colour surrounding, enveloping and glowing at these parts of your body.
- Follow your feelings and continue to bring your soothing

colour to different parts of your body as required. Notice how the colour soothes and relaxes.

- You can imagine your colour flowing into the positions of your chakras if you feel comfortable doing this. For example, as you inhale, imagine your soothing colour flowing into the centre of your chest. The centre of your chest is the location of your heart chakra.

- Some people find it helpful to imagine the colour as water. So, you can bath yourself in the colour and bring flowing coloured water or even the imagery of a coloured waterfall into areas of your body to visualise cleansing and healing for yourself.

- When you feel you have worked with your soothing colour sufficiently, simply rest in a state of relaxation for as long as you want. This visualisation is good to practice in bed before you go to sleep.

The Special Place Visualisation

This method requires you to imagine being at a place where you can feel relaxed and safe. Many people prefer to visualise a place they already know. Perhaps you have fond memories of a beach from a relaxing holiday, or perhaps the top of a hill you used to walk up when you were young, or perhaps a log cabin in a forest you stayed in once. What matters, is that this place is special to you in a way that it evokes feelings of serenity and peace. You could equally call this your sacred place, if you are more comfortable with this term.

Some people prefer to visualise a fictional place. In general, people feel most relaxed visualising themselves alone in beautiful nature scenes, but some people prefer to be indoors, and some people like the presence of other people or animals in their imaginings. Go with what works for you and perhaps you will be able to instantly decide on your special place or perhaps you will try a few different options before settling on it.

It is often beneficial to construct some sort of imagined journey that leads you to your special place, and this can be aligned with the process of winding down and more deeply relaxing. For example, if your special place is a beach, you can imagine yourself walking down some steps that wind down to your idyllic beach. Or if your special place is a cabin in a forest, you can imagine walking through the forest and then through the door into the cabin. As you take the journey towards your special place, slowly deepen your breathing and further and further relax.

The more you practice this relaxation technique, the faster you will be able to reach a state of deep relaxation, and you may get to the stage where you can relax very quickly and can therefore shorten the journey in your imagination to your special place.

Take some time to think through your journey and your special place. You may find it helpful to write down some pointers, but do allow yourself some room to be spontaneously creative within your imagination.

Method:

• Decide on your special place.
• Sit comfortably in a chair with your back and head supported or lay down in a comfortable position on your back. Ensure you are warm enough.
• Close your eyes and gradually slow and deepen your breathing rhythm.

- When you feel yourself beginning to further relax, imagine and visualise yourself walking towards your special place.
- When you arrive, enter your special place. And begin to imagine and visualise your special place. For example, if you are on a beach — see the colours of the water, hear the sounds of the waves, feel the sand beneath your feet, smell the fresh sea air, taste the salt — bring your awareness to what comes easiest for you to sense, and bring it to life.
- You can sit or lay down in your special place, you can walk around, or you could even visualise playing a sport, swimming or hiking. Whatever makes you feel relaxed and at peace.
- Don't worry about sustaining the visualisation and sensations of your special place. Simply allow your mind to drift as you would naturally do if you were actually there.
- When you are relaxed, you have access to more coherent mental processes. You may experience some useful realisations and gain clarity about certain situations in your life.
- If any worries or unpleasant thoughts disturb you, return your focus to your special place and concentrate on breathing slowly and deeply. You can say to yourself, "This is my special place and I feel safe here, and I am becoming more and more relaxed." It's best to observe your thoughts without reacting to them. Imagine them as clouds that come and go.
- Bask in the sensations and relaxing feelings evoked by your special place and stay for as long as you like.
- When you are ready to leave, you can imagine yourself walking away from your special place, back to your starting point, and then you can gradually come back into your physical awareness and open your eyes.

If you are prone to anxiety or trauma symptoms, you can bring this special place to your mind as necessary in your daily life — the thought of it will help you relax. It can also be helpful to draw your special place or collect images that represent it. Put them around your home and perhaps carry a small image in your wallet or purse. If you begin to feel distress, but thinking of your special place is not possible due to anxiety or situational factors, then simply look at the image, and the associations with relaxation will bring you towards feelings of safety and peace.

You can also create a short phrase, that is only known to you, that represents your special place. Each time you practice the special place relaxation technique, say the phrase in your mind at the start. If you begin to feel distress in daily life, then you can close your eyes and say the phrase to yourself. The resulting association will help to relax you. Example phrases could be, 'shimmering trees' or 'waves of peace' or 'mountain calm' or 'crystal cave'. Try and create a phrase that you are unlikely to hear anyone say in everyday life, as you want your phrase to remain associated only with your special place and the feelings of relaxation you've experienced.

Other relaxation techniques and tips:

There are numerous other methods for inducing relaxation and I list some examples here that are known to be highly effective:

• Use aromatherapy essential oils to relax. You can place them in a bath or place them with water into a diffuser to generate an aroma in your home or place of work. There are also aromatherapy misting sprays and roller balls you can purchase or make yourself. Rub the roller ball into your temples and the inside of your wrists. The most relaxing oils are lavender, valerian, chamomile, clary sage, marjoram, frankincense, rose, sandalwood and jasmine.

• There are many other breathing techniques, such as Pranayama and Kriya, that are slightly more complicated, but can be very relaxing and beneficial. You can easily find courses to go to or to purchase online.

• Regular meditation is profoundly beneficial for inducing relaxation, and the calming effects carry through into day to day life. I explain more about meditation in a later chapter.

• Spend time in nature. The natural elements, colours, sounds, smells can be very soothing and can bring harmony and relaxation. Be amongst the trees, swim in the sea or a river, walk in the wind, stand barefoot on the Earth. Sit in front of an open fire and appreciate the transformative energy.

• Gardening and any kind of work where you are getting your hands into the soil can be very grounding.

• Listen to music that relaxes you.

• Playing a musical instrument can also be very relaxing. Simply banging on a drum can relieve tension.

• Look at images and photos that bring you a sense of relaxation.

• Do something for yourself that is self-caring. Have a bath, brush your hair, cook a good meal, go for a walk. Any activity that you feel is self-nurturing and beneficial for your health and well-being will lead to heightened levels of relaxation.

• Talk to a good friend and socialise with people you feel good being with.

- Spend time with animals. Cats and dogs will often induce relaxation for people.

- Express yourself through a creative pursuit. Painting, photography, knitting, writing — the process of being creative induces relaxation.

- Chanting mantras either with your voice or in your mind can provide a single focus and the repetition will clear your thoughts. Slowly repeating the word 'Om' for five minutes can help to induce deep relaxation. To chant it, you would pronounce it, Aum, so it would sound more like, ahhuuooooommm. There are free tutorials online that can guide you. I do highly recommend singing mantras if you feel comfortable doing so.

- Express yourself with your voice. Sometimes, we need to get things out of our system that we have not expressed. In particular, if you feel a pent-up frustration, go out to nature or somewhere you are alone and let out a shriek or a roar! It can help sometimes to thump on your chest and make some gorilla noises. It may sound silly, but it can be very effective at releasing tension and stress. Sounds such as ooh, aah or eh, when vocalised somewhat forcefully can help to release unexpressed emotions and bodily tension.

- If you ever feel threatened, you can visualise yourself surrounded by a sphere of protective light. Some people find that imagining the sphere is spinning like a tornado around them, can be more effective. And some people expand the sphere outwards in a pulsing way. You can also imagine yourself holding a shield if you feel like you need protection. Whatever works best for you.

- Rolling your eyes can induce relaxation. So, you slowly roll your eyes up, then down, then left and then right — leaving them in each position for around 10 seconds.

- Learn about the acupressure points on your hands and face and you can then relieve tension by placing some light pressure with your finger tips on these points or by tapping with your fingers gently.

- Energy healing therapies can be very relaxing and can assist with alleviating stress and many other issues can also be resolved.

- Physical exercise is a good way to discharge stress and burn off emotions. There are some more relevant tips in the previous chapter Movement, Exercise and Bodywork.

- Cleaning up and organising your living and working spaces can help you to feel more relaxed.

- Organise your time so that you are aware of your schedule and don't feel over-rushed. And don't forget to schedule in some time for you to just relax!

CHAPTER SIX

Sleeping Well

People generally need between seven and nine hours sleep per night, although this can vary and some people are fine with much less. Broadly speaking, the older a person gets, the less sleep is required.

There are two main types of sleep that occur — one is to repair the body and one is to process the mind.

- Slow-wave sleep primarily functions to rejuvenate the body though repairing tissues, recharging the brain with glucose and performing a back log of maintenance tasks for the immune system.

- Dreaming sleep, otherwise known as Rapid Eye Movement (REM) sleep, primarily functions to process thoughts, emotional arousals and stress responses. In particular, dreaming serves to discharge emotional arousals that were not sufficiently acted upon or expressed during the day. The mind will often hold on to an expectation of action to fulfil instincts or emotions, and these expectations normally become deactivated during dreams where a simulation of action and expression occurs.

If a person spends a lot of time worrying and ruminating they will experience more time in REM sleep. And this pattern can have detrimental health consequences if it continues over a long period. This is because the person will receive less restorative sleep in terms of bodily repair, and will also deplete their motivational energy due to excessive dreaming. This means, they will wake up feeling physically and mentally exhausted, and this is very common for people who are depressed.

Therefore, excessive worrying and ruminating can not only impact the quality of your sleep, but also your health. I have provided information about how to overcome worrying in the later chapters entitled Overcoming Anxiety and Healing Depression.

Tips For Sleeping Well

If you occasionally have difficulty sleeping or sometimes wake up feeling tired — over the course of two weeks, take a note of your sleep patterns, your diet and also your lifestyle patterns. Look for any correlations that could reveal what is causing the sleep issues.

For example, you might notice you had a coffee after dinner twice in this two-week period and both of those nights, you didn't sleep very well. Perhaps you'll notice that if you watch more than two hours of television in the evening, you find it more difficult to get to sleep. Or maybe you will see a correlation between how late you were working on your computer and how tired you felt the next day. As you notice a correlation, do what you can to make appropriate changes, and see if you can resolve the issue.

What follows here is a list of practical tips for sleeping well. Everyone is different. You can experiment to find what works best for you:

• Ensure you do some movement and exercise during the day, but not within three hours of going to bed. Some gentle stretching before bed can be beneficial, but nothing too vigorous.

• Don't have any heavy protein after about 7pm — no red meat, cheese etc. Don't have any food or drink with high sugar, sweetener or caffeine contents after about 3pm.

• Get ready for bed at least an hour before you intend to be asleep. So, perhaps, brush your teeth, put on pyjamas or a dressing gown and wind down an hour before you actually go to bed.

• Lower stress levels and induce calmness by practicing relaxation techniques (see previous chapter Relaxation Techniques).

• Drink chamomile or lavender tea about two hours before bed time.

• About two hours before bed time, you could have a warm bath with around 20 drops of lavender essential oil added and some Epsom salt.

• If your bedroom receives light pollution, install black-out curtains or blinds. If that is not an option, buy a silk or cotton blindfold (eye mask) to wear when you sleep. The less light disturbance, the better your sleep will be. If you are afraid of the dark, ensure your night-light is not too bright and is orange in colour.

• Due to all the man-made light sources, sometimes our body and mind can lose a bearing on when the morning is and when the evening is. Another useful tip, is to go outside and look in the direction of the sun shortly after you get up in the morning. This helps to set up a beneficial circadian rhythm, so your body clock will then know when it is time to sleep.

- Do not watch television, listen to radio or spend time on electronic devices shortly before bed. It is recommended to have at least an hour of down-time before bed whereby you are not experiencing any significant stimulus. If you do have to be on your computer or phone until late, make sure you have 'night mode' activated or install an app such as f.lux that will automatically dull the blue light and turn the screen more orange as the sun goes down. Blue light is very stimulating and orange is more relaxing.

- Ensure it is quiet, don't leave radios or televisions on. Use earplugs if there is noise that disturbs you.

- Don't sleep with a mobile phone near your head. Turn off wi-fi and Bluetooth on all your devices. Do not sleep with any electric blankets plugged in.

- Ensure the temperature is right for you — not too hot and not too cold. Wool duvets regulate heat naturally. Yet, synthetic materials tend not to breathe well and can become too hot or cold. Ensure that any radiators in the bedroom are not set to make a significant temperature change during the night.

- Open windows and allow fresh air into your bedroom at least twice a week. If fresh air is not possible due to pollution, it may be worth investing in an air purifier. There are fanless and silent air purifiers you can purchase. Airfree is one make that I am familiar with. These purifiers can also help to prevent allergies such as hayfever, and therefore induce better sleep.

- Some people find standing on earth or grass for a few

minutes before going to bed can have a grounding and relaxing effect.

- Make a simple spray with lavender oil and water, and spray your pillows shortly before going to bed.
- Do not watch television or use devices when in bed. Maintain a sacred bedroom where you do not have any major stimulus.
- Dedicate your bedroom to relaxing and sleeping. In terms of furnishings and items, keep it soothing. Bright and vibrant colours can be over stimulating, but deep shades of either blue, green or red are usually conducive to sleep.
- Wash your bedding fabrics only with natural eco-friendly laundry products. The chemicals found in mainstream products can often act as stimulants. The same goes for personal hygiene and cosmetic products, they can also act as stimulants. Be mindful of what you use, especially if you take a shower or bath at the end of the day.
- Buy a new mattress if you feel uncomfortable. Natural latex mattresses come in a range of firmness and are usually the least toxic and most comfortable mattresses.
- You might be more comfortable using pillows stuffed with wool or kapok, instead of feather or polyester pillows that can inhibit breathing and cause over-heating. Also, consider the optimal firmness of your pillows. If a pillow is too firm or too soft this can create discomfort and disturb your sleep.
- You could try the old trick of eating a spoonful of raw honey with some Himalayan salt sprinkled on top shortly before bed.
- Calm yourself using deep breathing and repeat in your mind an affirmation such as, *"With each new breath I am drifting closer and closer to a deep and restorative sleep."*

- You can play minimal soothing music or a nature sounds audio for an hour to assist you to drift off to sleep. Many people find the sound of rain to be soothing.
- I don't recommend pharmaceutical sleeping pills, they can be harmful and often disrupt important dreaming processes. Take natural Valerian capsules if needed.
- Foods high in tryptophan can assist with sleep. Also, ensure you are receiving sufficient levels of vitamin B6, zinc, calcium and magnesium.
- Once in bed, go back through the day in your mind's eye. You'll probably find yourself pondering on certain events and that is good, as you'll process thoughts and emotions from the day. Often, you'll fall straight to sleep once you've gone through the day in your mind, and this will also help to lighten the load for your dream cycles.
- Some people prefer to write a journal or make an audio recording about their day before bed and this will serve the same purpose as above.
- If you are worrying about the next day, run through in your mind what you are planning, and perform a mental checklist of the preparations you have made and anything you will need to do the next day. You can also visualise what you plan to do and what you want to happen, and this can put your mind at ease. It can be beneficial to say a prayer or to affirm any goals and intentions you have. Feeling inspired and in control of your life will put you at ease.
- Sometimes, you will have ideas and inspirations in the period as you are drifting closer to sleep, and these ideas can ping you awake. If this is happening, keep a notepad and pen handy so you can make a note of your ideas. You will usually then be able to fall asleep soon afterwards.

• You don't want to keep reinforcing in your mind that your bed is a place where you do not sleep. So, if you can't sleep after about one hour, it is best to get up, leave your bedroom and do something. Don't eat anything, and do something mundane, so you're not rewarding yourself for not sleeping and not creating any major stimulus. Mop the floor, organise the filing cabinets, read a dull novel — any mundane task that doesn't create much excitement. Keep going until you are exhausted and have to sleep. Then, the key is, to always get up at exactly the same time, no matter how much sleep you've managed to get. Even on Sunday morning, get up at exactly the same time. Stick to this discipline and it will help you to fall asleep at the time you want.

CHAPTER SEVEN

Understanding Emotions

It is normal to experience a wide range of emotions in life. From sadness and grief, to joy and elation. Emotions serve a purpose. They are signals that reveal information about how we think and feel about ourselves and the experiences we have in life.

Emotions are often fleeting, coming and going like the wind as you manoeuvre your way through life. Yet, at times, it is beneficial to pay attention to your emotions and to make a conscious effort to recognise the information they provide. When we understand the messages behind our emotions, we can understand the causes of our emotions. We can recognise how emotions affect us, and then we can make choices to direct our life in a more fulfilling way.

You can try this exercise. Over the course of one week, monitor your emotions and take a note of what makes you feel happy, excited, joyful, sad, angry or frustrated. You could simplify this task and break it down into two columns —

positive emotions and negative emotions. What you are looking to identify in particular, is what you were thinking and doing at the time of the emotion.

At the end of the week, take a look at your list and try to evaluate what changes you could make in order to make your life easier. Often there are quite simple changes you can make to alleviate stress and negative emotion, or increase positive emotions.

Little things, such as, you might recognise you get stressed when rushing around in the morning and so you set your alarm clock earlier and go to bed earlier. Maybe you recognise that cooking on Sundays when your mother-in-law is visiting is always stressful, and so you book a table at a restaurant instead.

Perhaps you recognise that walking in the woods near your home makes you feel good, and so you set aside the time to do this more often. Maybe you realise that being with a certain friend is particularly joyful and you make an effort to arrange more time with this friend.

Changing your life circumstances to lessen negative emotions and increase positive emotions is often very simple. But sometimes, you do have to go through a process of identifying your emotions and recognising the reasons for them — then you can make changes based on your observations.

Reactions and Responses

How you react and respond to your life circumstances, determines the emotions you will experience. Ultimately, you have to accept, that you are the source of your own emotions.

People will often say, "My boss is driving me crazy." "My kids make me so angry." "The tax system is to blame for my misery." But in reality, it is their reactions that are causing their emotions. Maybe the boss is incredibly abrasive, maybe the kids are very mischievous, and maybe the tax system is unfair. Yet, how we react to these circumstances will directly relate to what emotions we experience when confronted by them.

What tends to happen, is people have all sorts of expectations, opinions and desires for how they want their life to be, and for how they want other people to treat them. Yet, when things go awry and not the way they want, they are faced with a contradiction that causes emotional reactions. So, their idea of contentment and happiness is dashed by what actually happens, and emotions such as anger, sadness, resentment, indignation and hopelessness can creep in. A person can then feel threatened and out of control.

How we emotionally react to certain situations often hinges on whether or not we feel contradicted or offended in some way. You may want the boss to be kind, the kids to be well behaved and the tax system to give you a break. But are these desires and expectations realistic? I'm not saying you should not have desires or expectations for what you want in life, but if you set yourself up so that your happiness depends on things always going as you want, inevitably, you are going to be disappointed.

You can try this exercise. Make a list of some instances when you reacted and felt negative emotions. Examples such as when you have felt offended, indignant, upset or annoyed. Take a look at your list and see if you can identify the reasons for your emotional reactions. How many of your reactions occurred due to your expectations, opinions, wants or desires being contradicted? Then, ask yourself, was it worth reacting in the way that you did?

Sometimes in life, emotional reactions are useful and serve a purpose, yet, much of the time, we waste valuable energy on reacting unnecessarily. We have to endure a certain amount of disappointment in life, and there will be times when our desires and expectations won't be fulfilled. But in many situations, you can free yourself from negative reactions simply by letting go of the desire to control, by letting go of the need to be right, and by letting go of the need to get what you want all the time.

Try not to lock yourself into too many desires and expectations. If the boss is abrasive, are you going to always let this upset you? If the kids are misbehaving, are you always going to react with anger? Is the tax bill always going to make you miserable? For your own peace of mind, you can lessen your reactions. You can lessen your desires, so that you are not so easily upset by other people's behaviours or by circumstances you find yourself in.

So, can you accept the boss is a monster, and not let it affect you? Can you join in and laugh and be mischievous with your kids at times? Can you accept that the tax system is run by a bunch of elitist crooks, and instead of being miserable about it, you accept that's the way it is, or you play their game and set up your company in an offshore tax haven, such as the Isle of Man?

The emotions you invest in your desires, will determine the emotions you experience if your desires are fulfilled or not fulfilled. The way to avoid the sting of emotional contradictions is to lessen your initial investment in the desire. So, you don't commit yourself to feeling a certain way if circumstances don't go as you want or expect.

For example, if a person is taking a driving test, they may

have already set themselves up with pre-meditated thoughts about how they will feel if they fail. They may say, "If I fail, it will be terrible and I'll be so upset." So, the emotional reaction has already been pre-loaded and is ready to be fired. Alternatively, they could say, "If I fail the test, it'll be a bit of a set-back, but ultimately I'll end up a better driver." In other words, they keep their emotional expectations at a minimum and are willing to accept what happens, and can also see a positive outcome.

The less you yearn for something to happen or worry about something not happening — the less you will be affected by negative emotions when things don't go as you want. It is healthy to have aspirations and hopes, but sometimes you have to recognise when yearning and worrying is weighing you down and causing negative emotions. And it is these negative emotions that can end up causing delays. On some occasions, you just need to accept that things take longer than you would like. It is often a good idea to loosen the time frame of your desires.

If you are frequently focused on what you desire, but have not got it yet, then try to desire less and be grateful for what is going well in your life. Sometimes, we simply need to accept where we are in life and lower our ambitions for a short while. This grants us inner peace; away from negativity generated by too much striving and worrying. When you can accept your life circumstances, then you will feel in control, and can be content.

You have to find a balance in life, whereby you can be relatively content whether you are making the progress you want or not. By recognising the detriments of negative thinking and emotional reactions, you can begin to value your own inner peace. You can become less judgemental and reactive, and be more resilient and steadfast.

Once you eliminate the unnecessary emotional reactions, you can better appreciate the circumstances that evoke emotions of a more profound nature. Many of our deeper feelings occur without any discernible mental reactions. For example, the ineffable joy you may feel when watching a sunset, the elusive inspiration you may feel when looking at a piece of art, or the mysterious elation you may feel when you are with your lover. Without the mind reacting with opinion or intellectual commentary; you can still experience feelings and emotions.

However, we often become conditioned to label our experiences in a binary way — seeing the world through a lens of either good or bad, right or wrong, successful or unsuccessful. And the thing is, if you operate mostly within this framework in terms of how you appraise yourself and your life circumstances, you'll be prone to negative emotions more often.

I grew up in England and people there often talk about the weather in these terms. They will say, "It's awful this rain today isn't it, so miserable." Or "It's such a lovely day, wonderful sunny weather." Yet, these assertions come from an idea that happiness is equated with being in the sun and misery is equated with being in the rain. If you live in England, that means you are going to do much of your life in misery! And many do.

Many people go through their lives evaluating circumstances in this binary way, and they bounce around between feeling good or bad, happy or sad, stressed or relaxed, satisfied or disappointed. What I recommend to people, is to become more of an observer of life rather than an evaluator. To have less and less opinion and judgement, and to more and more move through life without mentally reacting to it.

o many aspects of life, such as the weather, that
control. And so it is rather futile to be weighed
tional reactions if there is nothing we can do
ning yourself to not react about people and
...stances that you can't control or change, you free
yourself of unnecessary emotional baggage. By simply
deciding not to evaluate and judge, you can remain neutral.
Then, it won't matter to you whether it is sunny or raining,
you are content with either. And besides, there is usually
another solution, such as an umbrella!

Try this. Write down all the things that worry you,
concern you or irritate you. Then look at this list and cross
off everything that you have no control over. What is left on
the list is what you can choose to accept or to take action to
resolve. To neutralise negative reactions, you have to either
accept your circumstances, or take action to resolve them.
But if you remain stuck in negative reactions, you will be
burdened by emotions.

A useful step to take in getting to this neutrality, is to
monitor your thoughts and reactions in a way that
neutralises negative emotions from taking hold. For example,
we need rain for the crops to grow and to replenish the
reservoirs and springs that we drink from — rain is a great
blessing. This type of positive interpretation serves to
counter any negative connotations that may arise from
negative thinking patterns. When you are able to accept
what happens in life, and also when possible see a bright
side, then you will become much more resilient.

The same can be applied to emotional reactions we have
about other people. For example, the boss at work — are they
under pressure and abrasive because of their own
insecurities and worries? If you can recognise the reasons for
other people's emotions, it allows you to be more

understanding, and you can then become less prone to reacting to them. This is not to say you should always be passive, as being assertive is at times necessary. But you can avoid taking things personally by recognising the reasons for other people's emotions.

Let's look at an example of a road rage reaction. Perhaps a driver veered in front of you recklessly on the motorway and you ended up feeling anger and resentment. During the time this driver was veering in front of you, you were concentrating on braking and slowing down, your body had reacted in a way to put you into a survival situation. Your blood pressure increased, cortisol and adrenaline were released, and your breathing quickened. After you'd slowed down and the situation was made safe, you then began to think about what happened. You felt anger and rage towards the other driver.

This driver defied your expectations and desires about safe driving, they were reckless, and it is natural to feel offended by this. But once it was clear there was no threat to your survival, you could have chosen to calm yourself. You could have counteracted the physical responses with slow deep breathing, and counteracted the mental responses by not thinking or speaking about the situation in an emotionally charged way.

You could have rationalised that maybe the driver was tired, under pressure and running late — you could have accepted what happened and been grateful no accident occurred. You could also have pulled over at a service station and taken a little walk around the car park. Physical exercise can be a good catharsis to discharge emotions and deactivate the fight or flight mechanism.

There are times in life when emotional reactions serve a purpose. I am not suggesting you become a Zen monk or nun that remains completely unperturbed in all circumstances. But many people do not neutralise their emotional reactions and this can lead to a build-up of stress and negativity, and potentially cause issues such as depression or anxiety.

The unfortunate aspect of our primitive fight or flight survival mechanism, is that it can also become activated when there is a threat to our happiness, status or sense of control. I talk more about this in the later chapter Overcoming Anxiety.

Resolving Emotional Cycles

People often exacerbate their emotions by thinking about themselves negatively. For example, they might believe their feelings of sadness are an indication of weakness or they might end up feeling guilty after an outburst of anger.

Another way people exacerbate their emotions is by thinking negatively about situations or other people. For example, an initial reaction of frustration may turn into rage if it is intensified by negative thoughts spawned by indignation, blame and resentment.

Try to recognise when your thought processes and mental reactions are generating further emotions. If you don't compound your emotions with negative reactions, you will be in a much better position to resolve your initial emotions.

I will go through some common emotional cycles in this section and suggest some solutions to resolve them.

If you think you've done something wrong, something that does not concur with your ethics and the values you adhere to, then you will likely react with guilt and shame. This is normal, and these emotions are providing you with information. Guilt and shame can be very helpful in providing you with instructions for being a better person. Via these emotions you can learn the lessons from your actions. You can affirm to yourself that you will take heed, and will do things differently in the future. Then you can forgive yourself, accept what happened and the emotions of guilt and shame will naturally dissipate.

Sometimes a process of atonement can also help to resolve emotions of guilt or shame. For example, if you were unkind to someone in the past, you can resolve this by apologising and being kind to them. And if you are no longer in touch with the person you were unkind to, you can make up for it by being kind to other people. If you were unfair in business and cheated someone out of their money, you can apologise and pay them back. And if you are not in touch with this person, you can give a homeless person the money.

It can be helpful to go through some process of redemption in order to forgive one's self and move on. But you do have to accept the past and stop judging yourself, in order to grant yourself the opportunity to atone. We do not need to punish ourselves through debilitating emotional cycles — we only need to recognise the messages in our emotions, take heed, take action and move on.

Anger and frustration are usually linked to some form of loss or the possibility of loss. Look to identify the loss and see if you can accept what has happened or might happen. Injustice does happen and sometimes there is nothing we can do about it. Try to come to terms with the loss and not compound emotions with irrational thinking and negative self-talk. If you can't accept the loss, come up with a strategy to recover your loss or compensate for it, and then take action. Try and channel frustration into being proactive. If you become angry at other people, it is usually best to walk away before any further confrontation occurs. Take some time alone and calm yourself.

Sadness is usually linked to feelings of dissatisfaction, apathy and helplessness. Look to identify what you can accept, let go of, or release from your life in order to move on. Sometimes a positive ritual is beneficial to say goodbye to someone or to mark the end of something in your life. You could write a letter saying goodbye and then bury the letter or watch it float away on a river. You could collect certain belongings you associate with what you want to let go of, and give them away or burn them on a fire. These kinds of positive rituals can be very helpful to symbolically demark changes you want to make. Then, look for what you can focus on, change, and bring rejuvenation to in your life.

Grief is an emotion that occurs when a person gradually processes a situation that causes great sorrow. There are circumstances in life, such as the death of a loved one, where emotions of sadness can develop into grief, and these emotions should not be fraught with attempts of suppression or with self-criticism. By making a conscious effort to accept your emotions, you can allow them to take a natural course. You can allow them to ebb and flow naturally and then dissipate.

If you feel overwhelmed by grief, it is best to manage it by dedicating a period of time each day to your sorrows. Thirty minutes or one hour is usually sufficient, and in this time, you think and emote about who or what you grieve for. It is a dedication — a positive ritual — and it will help you process the grief. You will know when it is time to make the dedication less frequent.

Resentment and bitterness are often formed due to blame. Blame locks you into a conflict with other people. You avoid blame by accepting the situation and by taking responsibility for your life. You do what you can to move on.

Even if people have mistreated you or betrayed your trust — blaming them and holding resentment is futile, and will only bring you into further emotional reactions. You will feel much stronger when you let go of blame.

Consistent worrying can lead to a sense of despair, confusion and hopelessness. You have to compose yourself with relaxation, then, look to see if there is anything you can do about your worries to alleviate them.

Write down what you could do and either do it immediately or schedule a time when you will do it. So, you could write down what the problem is, brainstorm solutions, evaluate the pros and cons of each solution, and decide what you will do. Taking action or making a plan to take action will release you from the burden of worrying.

If you realise there is nothing you can do, and what you are worrying about is out of your control, it is best to disengage your mind and to not think any further about it.

It can also help to focus on the positive things in your life that you are grateful for. Do you have a home, food in the fridge and water? When you count your blessings and make an effort to appreciate what you have right now in the present moment, this can alleviate negative emotions and worries.

By discussing your emotions with people you trust, you can express your feelings honestly and openly, and this can diffuse any further build up. Receiving feedback and advice from people can help you to understand your emotions and provide useful information. Ideally, you want to talk with someone who can empathise, and also provide encouragement, hope and perspective, rather than simply wallow in your emotions with you. It is usually not helpful to publicise your worries and emotional states on social media.

Emotional Processing

What follows is a step by step exercise designed to assist people to accept, understand and process their emotions.

Many of our emotions are entirely normal and they will naturally dissipate over time. This is not an exercise designed to suppress emotions, but rather to process them with self-compassion and resolve. Some of the steps may not be relevant for you, and so you can skip them as appropriate.

Please note. If you are struggling with highly distressing emotions due to a traumatic experience, you should not attempt this exercise unless you are confident you can induce yourself into a relaxed state if required.

I recommend doing this exercise at the end of the day before you go to sleep or during a meditation session.

• Firstly, turn towards the emotions. Acknowledge and recognise the emotions you are feeling.

• Allow yourself to feel and get in touch with the emotions.

• Calm yourself by slowing and deepening your breathing. As best as you can, don't think critically about the emotions.

• See if you can trace back to the original reason for your emotion and also look to see if any other emotions have developed since. Take some time to explore and define any different emotions you feel.

• Just allow yourself to move through the memories and any emotions you feel, without thinking about them critically. Try to allow your mind to only observe your emotions and not react to them.

• Then focus your attention on understanding what each emotion is revealing about yourself. What are the messages in the emotions telling you? Can you learn anything from these emotions?

- Are there any ways in which you could neutralise these emotions by changing your desires, opinions or expectations? Can you make peace with yourself? Can you make peace with others?
- Can you accept what happened and let it be? Are there any actions you could take to bring a sense of closure to these emotions?
- Is there an outcome that you are afraid of? Is there a worst-case scenario you imagine? If so, is there anything you could do to alleviate these fears? Can you make peace with uncertainty, knowing that you have done all you can?
- Acknowledge anything you have learnt from the emotions and take note if there are any changes you intend to make.

Occasionally, another layer of emotion can become perceptible later on. If this happens, you can take the time to repeat the process.

Sometimes, it only requires a simple realisation and we can click our fingers to process and let go of an emotion. But other times, the process will take longer. Don't get frustrated with yourself if emotions persist. Keep yourself relaxed and free of negative thinking as much as possible. Accept your emotions as a part of your inner guidance system. Look for the messages in your emotions. Understanding emotions is the key to moving through them and beyond.

CHAPTER EIGHT

Healing Depression

During the course of life, it is natural to go through times of sadness. For example, it is natural to grieve, and it is natural to sometimes have regrets, worries and fears. But these times when we feel in a depressed mood, should not be considered as a depression, unless the feelings continue to dominate over a long period.

It is important to realise that it is not circumstances that lead to depression; it is the way a person responds to circumstances that leads to depression. And therefore, preventing depression is largely about learning to manage emotions and control thinking processes.

Depression is normally caused by excessive worrying over some form of loss. This excessive worrying can manifest due to prolonged sentiments of regret, shame, guilt, grief, resentment, indignation, anxiety and anger — and it is usually a combination. If a person does not come to terms with their life circumstances and begin to deal with the implications, they can become preoccupied with negative thoughts. This preoccupation with negativity results in a depressed mood and the depletion of motivational energy.

Depression is essentially a strong and protracted emotion that locks a person's attention into negative thoughts and feelings. Because a depressed person is in a near constant state of emotional arousal they are operating mostly from the more primitive part of the brain — the part of the brain that is rather binary in its functioning and deals with the fight or flight mechanism.

This explains why depressed people often become limited in their range of thinking processes. Access to their neo-cortex, the more evolved part of the brain responsible for reasoning and rational thinking, has become restricted. For example, if a person is divorced, they may become convinced that because their spouse left them, their life is meaningless and they will never find another partner. Yet, these are extreme thoughts and irrational interpretations, typical of a mind restricted by emotional arousal.

If this type of irrational and narrow-minded thinking continues, it can lead to the generation of more worries and more emotions, and it can quickly become a vicious cycle. Such emotional turmoil can then lead to a situation where everything in life becomes difficult due to negative thinking and the expectation of things going wrong and becoming worse.

People who enter into these states of depression often become very self-absorbed and self-centred. They can act as if the world revolves around them and they will often interpret events very personally, getting stuck in self-blame, regret and guilt. They often have an irrational view of how pervasive a problem is in their life, and become mired by negative emotions, self-pity and victimhood. So, they can find it difficult to perceive any neutral or positive interpretations. They also often lose a rational perspective on time, thinking that one bump in the road will lead to a lifetime of trouble.

You may be thinking of skipping this chapter if you aren't depressed, but there are useful tips here that can be applied to preventing depression. And you could also use this information to understand and assist people you may know who are suffering with depression.

How to Heal Depression

If you are depressed, you should not spend too much time digging unnecessarily into your memories of past events. Although, it can be useful to identify the origins of your depression, and recognise what has changed about your life since that time. By acknowledging how events of the past have affected you, you can begin the process of coming to terms with what occurred. You can start to move forward by embarking on a journey of acceptance and resolution.

So, you could write down what happened and how it made you feel. And then also write down what has changed in your life since. This may sound simplistic, but many people with depression never actually think back and identify what was happening in their life around the time their depressed mood began. In particular, what you are looking to identify is how your life has changed since the depression began. If you can determine the factors involved, you can use this information to your advantage to build a strategy to accept what happened, and to rectify what is causing discontentment.

To start the process of accepting what happened in the

past, begin by asking yourself the question, "What is stopping me from accepting this?" Bring your awareness to your answers and acknowledge what happened and how it made you feel. Then remind yourself that these events are in the past. You cannot change the past and yet you can change how you feel about the past. And it is always beneficial to let go of past emotions that are no longer serving any purpose. By simply acknowledging what has happened and how it made you feel, you can begin to ease the pain associated with this past upset, and you can begin to process these emotions and move forward.

Depression is often exacerbated because people make choices that lead to further dissatisfaction. So, they make choices that result in a reduction of situations that could provide them with emotional and social fulfilment. For example, people with depression will often stop doing activities that they used to enjoy, they will often stop looking after their health, disengage from people, isolate themselves, lose motivation to work, and stop challenging themselves. And due to their attention being locked into their misery, they frequently fail to perceive that these changes are perpetuating their depression; regressing them into a further sense of inadequacy and hopelessness.

Take a look at what you have identified as having changed in your life since the depression began. Then ask yourself the question, "What would I be doing differently if I wasn't depressed?" From your answers, make an effort to develop a strategy consisting of small steps that are focused on re-engaging with life and re-gaining fulfilment. In other words, once you have identified what used to make you feel happy before the depression, seek ways to re-introduce these activities and patterns into your life.

As with all creatures, human beings have inherent needs.

Beyond physical survival needs, we have emotional and social needs that are in many ways just as essential to our well-being. If you are not sure what is causing your discontentment and depressed mood, have a think about the social and emotional aspects of your life.

For example, do you feel safe in the environments in which you live and work? Do you feel satisfied with what you are doing in your life? Do you feel you have control and autonomy in your life? Do you have someone you can trust and confide in? Do you have any connections in a wider community? Is there someone you can be intimate with? Are you doing anything in life that gives you a sense of meaning and achievement? Do you feel recognised and accepted for who you are? What is it that you feel is lacking in your life?

It is often futile to simply say, "I want to be happier" as you have to identify what will make you happier and then develop a specific action plan to move yourself in this direction.

- If you want to be happier, you have to unpack that sentiment by exploring answers to the question, what would make you happier? For example, perhaps doing an activity you used to enjoy will make you feel happier.

- You want to feel safer? Unpack that, what would make you feel safer? For example, perhaps finding a different place to live will make you feel safer.

- You want to feel more satisfied with what you are doing in life? Perhaps look for a different job, hobby or training in a new skill.

- You feel lonely? Could you ring up an old friend and arrange to meet them or join a new class or group?

- You feel worthless? Could you go and help someone you know or volunteer for a charity?

• You feel inadequate and hopeless? Could you go and accomplish something? Perhaps you could clear out the garage, learn a new skill, walk the dog, cook something new or redecorate your bedroom.

So, you can make a list of your difficulties and what you feel dissatisfied about in life. Then you can be proactive and look for solutions. You can think of practical steps you could take to bring about positive changes in your life. Your strategy is simply to re-engage with life and gain some feelings of fulfilment.

Try to be clear with what you want and specific about your objectives. Make your steps achievable and start with small changes, and as you succeed in those, you will find renewed vigour to move forward to greater steps. You will likely have to push through some resistance during this process, but it will be worth it! If at all possible, discuss your plans with at least one person you trust and hopefully they can assist you to develop your strategy and work towards it.

Central to your success is to direct your attention outwards. So, you seek activities that occupy your mind, giving yourself less and less time to worry and ruminate. The keys are, to keep active, productive and social. Work towards your goals, refine your strategy, keep moving forward, just small steps to start with. And remember, it is helpful sometimes to lower your expectations and ambitions, and find appreciation from the small things in life. It might be best to let go of your major aspirations for a little while and focus on small steps to increase your sense of well-being.

Sometimes, people can become so overwhelmed by social pressures, that they become obsessed by material consumption and the elevation of status. But this can lead to a lifestyle devoid of happiness and joy. Be mindful of the differences between your needs and your desires. Don't bother to compare yourself to anyone or get upset if you can't manifest your ideal life in the next few weeks. Be patient and persevere, and try to enjoy the journey and not be too over-focused on the destination of your desires.

Find peace within yourself by appreciating what you do have. Be grateful for all the things that have gone well in your life. By practicing gratitude regularly, you will enter into a state of humility that will neutralise negative thoughts and emotions. Make a list of all the people, experiences and things that you are grateful for and keep this list updated. At least twice a week update your gratitude list.

The more you move away from self-absorption the better. It will be good for you to do things with others and to be of service to others, it doesn't matter how small. Try to interact more frequently with the people in your life, your friends, family and colleagues. If you don't have a job where you work with others, perhaps consider doing some charity or volunteering work. Maybe you could learn a new skill, and signing up to a course will likely lead you to meet new people and develop social connections. Any social stimulation that brings you out of negative thinking will be helpful.

Doing anything that is new and novel can give you a positive boost. People thrive when they are challenged by new experiences, new knowledge and the learning of new skills. This leads to increased confidence and a sense of achievement. Depression can be caused or prolonged by the trappings of mundaneness. Doing something new can really help you to move beyond the mundane. You could go on a trip to somewhere you've never been, play a sport you've never tried, or just get on a bus you've never been on and see where it goes. Begin to see life as an interesting adventure. Be spontaneous at times and if you like something, great, if you don't, it's okay. The very act of seeking novel experiences will boost your confidence and make you feel better, even if sometimes you don't entirely enjoy what you end up doing.

As you continue to build on your strategy and re-engage with life; a sense of meaning and purpose will emerge from your efforts and will provide additional momentum to your progress. What often helps people, is to become part of something bigger than themselves. And it doesn't need to be anything world changing. Some examples include, joining a gardening group, a Tai Chi class, a weekly meditation gathering, a choir — it doesn't really matter as long as it provides some sense of working with others towards progress and achievement. Remember to recognise the actions you take that boost your mood the most, and then incorporate more of these types of activities into your life.

People with depression often have low levels of self-esteem, and it is important that they remind themselves of their successes, talents, abilities, skills and achievements. Everyone has them and sometimes people can lose sight of how valuable they are. They can overlook how they've cared for people, raised children, held down jobs, completed educational courses, looked after a home. Even so called negative qualities can begin to be re-envisioned. For example, if a person is overly analytical, they can accept this and apply it to analysing their strategy to move forward in life! Focus on your strengths and begin to give yourself credit for your achievements in life, and this will reinforce your momentum in moving forward.

With regard to your neurochemistry. Serotonin is linked to mood and dopamine is linked to motivation. Serotonin is boosted through exercise, sunlight, socialising, intimacy and caring for others. Dopamine is boosted through the completion of tasks, a sense of achievement and taking time to care for yourself.

Low levels of these neurotransmitters are found in people with depression, and in the vast majority of cases, this is caused by prolonged depressive thinking and feeling. What a person thinks and feels actually makes a physical impression on their brain. In many regards, your neurochemistry is a mirror of your thoughts and feelings, and will change accordingly. The more you reinforce positive attributes to your inner mind, the more beneficial neural pathways will be forged and reinforced. In other words, the more you appreciate yourself and the people and experiences in your life, the more your neurochemistry will make beneficial changes.

Getting a good night's sleep is often difficult for people with depression. This is because the more a person worries and ruminates, the more the brain has to dream, which then leads to less recuperative slow wave sleep. This is why people with depression invariably feel tired on waking. All mental expectations and emotional arousals that are not acted upon have to be discharged somehow, and action within the dream state is one way we have evolved to deal with this equation.

Ultimately, the solution is to reduce worrying and ruminating so there is less arousal to be discharged through dreams, thus allowing more time for restorative slow wave sleep. Whilst this goal is being worked towards, anyone with depression should be mindful to not sleep too much. It may seem counter-intuitive, but by setting an alarm early, you can ensure you don't deplete your motivational energy (dopamine) through excessive dreaming. Some form of outdoor daily exercise will also be helpful and will increase blood flow to the brain whilst raising serotonin and dopamine levels.

It can be a helpful practice to constrain worrying and ruminating into a certain time of the day. For example, you could do a thirty-minute worry session in the mornings. And if any negative thinking or worrying starts later in the day, you are assertive with yourself and think, "I will not worry about this now, if necessary I will worry about it tomorrow morning." You can combine your worry session with some relaxation practices and gradually you can turn this session into a productive meditation. Never worry for more than half an hour a day! That's the secret to preventing and healing depression.

At times, you will have to challenge your negative thoughts and you will have to make an effort — to change focus, to stop replaying negative thoughts, to engage your rational senses and to question your negativity. Ask yourself, "What good is this thinking doing?" It is normal to have some self-disapproval and discontentment at times. But in order to attain inner peace we have to accept our circumstances, learn from our experiences and then move on. Otherwise, we can end up languishing in the limbos of regret, guilt, frustration or unworthiness. The silver lining is always in the wisdom we learn through our experiences, that we can then apply in the future.

If you find yourself thinking negatively, then challenge your thoughts, are they rational? Can you see things from a different perspective? Try and come up with alternative viewpoints that are neutral or positively affirming. Weigh things up with a more balanced and rational thought process and undo the deceptions of your emotions. Praise yourself for the progress you are making and remind yourself that things will pass, change is natural.

Eliminate doom from your language. For example, instead of saying, "I can't bear it anymore" say, "I am now ready to make changes to help myself." Use your inner dialogue in a way that builds your confidence to see things through. And also builds your expectation that you can adapt and change.

If people around you are depressed, they may have a detrimental effect on your progress. You should ensure to balance your company so that you are also spending time with people who are productive, active and social. But also, do remember to take responsibility for your thoughts and actions, and don't fall into blaming other people and circumstances.

If you face criticism from others, always admit any mistakes you may have made up front, and then let go of thoughts about the criticism as best you can. If you do feel a sense of injustice — without being defensive or aggressive, calmly stand up for yourself, and challenge the basis of the criticism. Sometimes, other people can be very disparaging for no good reason. You have to do your best to not let it drag you down, whilst also being assertive if appropriate. Without boasting or being needy for attention, it is often helpful to push the value you have for yourself outwards so that other people become aware of your standing. Sometimes in life, if you don't let people know what you want, how you feel, and what you have to offer, they can overlook your needs or perceive you as weak and take advantage of you.

Negative thoughts and feelings are often intensified by a misuse of imagination. People with depression tend to fantasise about nebulous fears of the future or dwell on replaying the past in ever more self-depreciating ways. These traits take them out of the present moment and because the emotional part of the brain cannot distinguish between imagined and real scenarios, they can end up generating more emotions and negativity, that then spill out into their actual life.

Instead of using your imagination as a misery simulator, where you rehearse your suffering, regrets, worries, fears, anxieties — try rehearsing success, try rehearsing ways in which you overcome your difficulties and go beyond your worries. Practice thinking about and visualising doing things that are beneficial to you. For example, if you are afraid of your driving test. Visualise yourself driving really well and passing the test and being happy about it. Obviously, you'll have to practice driving in the real world also, but visualising your life going as you want has been proven to be an effective strategy for positive change. It will imbue you with more confidence and alleviate worrying.

Laughter is a powerful medicine and if you're getting stuck in negative emotions, think of the funniest moments in your life. Ring up a friend and re-live a funny memory and laugh. Also, remember to laugh at yourself, it is healthy to joke about yourself and laugh — don't take life too seriously!

Learning techniques to relax is imperative. Calmness will initiate a more rational perspective and enable you to break free of cycles of negative thinking. It will also reduce levels of cortisol and increase the efficiency of your immune system. Take regular breaks and be aware of your stress levels, and implement relaxation practices as needed. Be careful to not over stimulate your mind with too much media consumption. And never underestimate how important time in nature is to your mental well-being. Fresh air, sunlight and the soothing colours and sounds of the natural world are mood enhancing, calming and healing.

Sometimes, places, people, thoughts, even a song or a smell can cause an association with a memory linked to the cause of your depression. You may consciously realise or it could happen unconsciously and you suddenly find yourself in a low mood for no apparent reason. You have to be mindful of this possibility and monitor yourself. It is a good idea to develop ways to defuse any triggers. By having response strategies of relaxation techniques and positive activities you can instigate, you can keep yourself calm and focused away from any negative thoughts and emotions that may arise. The more you defuse your triggers, the less they will occur, until eventually they will cease to happen.

Be sure to drink plenty of clean water and eat well. In particular, avoid excess sugar and processed foods. Ensure you are getting enough B vitamins, chromium, folic acid and omega 3. Take good quality supplements as necessary. Also, foods containing tryptophan such as cashew nuts are excellent natural anti-depressants. I talk more about mood boosting foods and supplements in the later chapter Nutrition For Your Mind.

An estimated 75% of people with depression recover within six months with no treatment at all. It is clear, that the majority of people are capable of resolving their own issues. And the information I've provided here in this chapter has been proven to help people resolve and heal depression quickly.

Therapy can help, but it is not recommended to see a counsellor or psychotherapist who wants to over-explore your past, as this can end up creating more impressions of misery in your mind. I suggest you avoid psychoanalytical and psychodynamic therapists. Go for someone who wants to focus more on the present time and is willing to help you get your life back on track. A good therapist can help with changing your attributional style of thinking, shifting your focus away from your emotions, guiding you to resolve difficulties in your life, and teaching you beneficial life skills.

In terms of taking medication such as anti-depressants, research clearly demonstrates, people who recover from depression without taking psychiatric medication are less likely to have a relapse. Mounting evidence is also revealing that psychiatric drugs often perpetuate, worsen and even create mental health problems. If you are taking anti-depressants, consider talking to your doctor about coming off the pills. But come off them very slowly, slower than the doctor will usually advise. For example, instead of going down in dose by half a pill, go down by a sixth of a pill at each stage. By doing this, you will allow your neurochemistry to adjust more gradually, and then you can come off these medications whilst minimising withdrawal symptoms.

You should also be aware that many pharmaceuticals given for heart problems, high cholesterol, migraines and other conditions have been found to cause depression in some people. If you don't know why you are depressed and are taking medication, you should definitely speak with your doctor about stopping or changing to different medications.

CHAPTER NINE

Overcoming Anxiety

The term anxiety is used to describe a wide variety of symptoms ranging from a persistent feeling of unease, to more severe feelings of distress that can lead to panic.

Underlying all types of anxiety are excess levels of stress. The keys to overcoming anxiety are found through managing stress arousal and redesigning lifestyle to prevent stress.

Firstly, it is important to recognise that stress has a natural purpose and is part of a natural reaction inherent to all humans. We need to feel some stress to know which situations are potentially threatening, so that we can take appropriate action. For example, if we are walking through a dangerous neighbourhood it is natural to experience some elevated levels of alertness and vigilance — and this stress serves to keep us ready to act to any perceived threat.

Everyone experiences some stress in their life and this can build up and turn into anxiety, but this anxiety is usually released when, for example, the walk through the dangerous neighbourhood is over, the exam has finished, the driving test is done or when the mother-in-law has gone home.

It is actually very common for people to experience anxiety before something they enjoy or find meaningful, such as playing a sports game, going on a first date or making a speech at a wedding. Once the game is played, the date is over or the speech is finished, the vast majority of people feel a sense of relief, and the stress and anxiety quickly fades.

How a person interprets their stress and anxiety is important. Unless there is a life-threatening situation, it is a good practice to think of any anxiety inducing situation as a challenge and *not* a threat. This is because the stress response that leads to anxiety is formed from the activation of the fight or flight mechanism.

The fight or flight mechanism evolved to protect us from threats to our survival and is enacted by the older part of the brain, in particular, the amygdala. It is still very valuable and necessary for survival. Sometimes, thinking processes and rational reasoning would be an impediment, and we need raw emotional signals to get us quickly out of danger. For example, if you're in the middle of a busy road with a bus coming straight for you, you don't have time to ponder about whether the bus will narrowly miss you or not, you just need to act and get out of the way.

When initiated, the fight or flight mechanism causes a fast release of hormones, and this in turn, leads to a number of physiological changes to help cope with demands. We breathe faster to get more oxygen to the blood, our blood pressure rises to increase circulation to muscles, and our digestion is interrupted to conserve energy.

The issue for the modern human, is that the processing involved with this survival mechanism is rather primitive and cannot differentiate between a psychological threat and a survival threat.

A survival threat can easily be realised and acted upon. For example, if you run away from a danger, you burn off the stress hormones during the action of running, and when you are safe, the fight or flight mechanism is deactivated. On the other hand, a psychological threat is often not acted upon and sometimes is not actually even realised. For example, an angry boss at work may cause you to become stressed, but you don't want to fight or flee the boss as you don't want to lose your job. But because this stress can activate the fight or flight mechanism, if no action is taken, the mechanism is not deactivated and an expectation of action can remain in place.

The stress hormones released during an activation of the fight or flight survival mechanism can cause fear, apprehension and anger. And these are the emotional responses that evolved for fighting or fleeing. The mechanism is then further compounded if a person begins to cycle through negative thoughts about the stressful situation. The negative thoughts perpetuate the emotions; leading to a continued release of stress hormones.

Anxiety is usually the result of a stress response not being released, that is further compounded by elements of the fight or flight mechanism remaining active.

The good news is that there are ways to manage stress arousal and overcome anxiety. And if you have anxiety, it is helpful to understand that stress and anxiety are natural and serve a purpose. So, you can now let go of any fears about you being ill, weak or crazy! All that has happened, is a natural survival function has gotten overloaded and is stuck on overdrive.

How do you overcome anxiety?

It can be very helpful to assess what it is in your life that is causing anxiety. In particular, to become aware of any specific triggers for your anxiety. Over the course of one week, take note of what you feel is causing anxiety. And maybe you don't know exactly why anxiety is occurring, but write down — what you were doing, what you were about to do, what you were thinking about, who you were in communication with and where you were. This is a task designed to help you discover the specific elements of your life that are causing stress and anxiety. Once you understand more about your patterns of anxiety, you can then make changes to help yourself.

As a start, you can prepare yourself with relaxation techniques prior to and also during any situation you recognise causes you anxiety. For example, if you feel stress and anxiety prior to and during a visit from your mother-in-law, you can practice a relaxation technique shortly before she arrives, and you can do some breathing practices during the visit to manage your stress levels. So, you are preparing yourself by becoming as relaxed as possible before the anxiety inducing situation and, as is required, you manage your stress levels with a relaxing breathing technique during the situation. Also, by doing some aerobic exercise after the situation, in this example, when the mother-in-law leaves, you can discharge stress hormones and release anxiety.

Stress and anxiety can cause a person to feel out of control and this feeling of being out of control can then further generate stress and anxiety. As you become more adept at controlling your stress levels, you will feel less and less anxiety. And you can over time get to the stage where, for example, you do not need to take such steps to alleviate anxiety before, during, or after a visit from your mother-in-law. By successfully managing your stress responses in situations that caused you anxiety, you train yourself to not have a stress response. You prove to yourself that the situation is no longer a threat as you can handle it.

It is important to recognise when a situation or relationship is causing you stress, and to then decide what action to take, to do something about it. Many situations and relationships cause people stress, but in most cases this stress can be managed and alleviated through relaxation techniques, breathing practices and aerobic exercise. But if you cannot manage to control your stress levels, the stress response can build up and lead to anxiety.

You have to recognise your limits and take action to protect yourself. Maybe you will need to eliminate anxiety causing situations from your life and take actions such as — move out of a home, end a relationship, leave a job or take a break and get some time alone. The more you are able to manage or vanquish the stress in your life, the more satisfaction and fulfilment you will feel. And these positive feelings will alleviate anxiety.

If a person feels an ongoing discontentment about their life, this can build up as stress and generate anxiety. This cumulation of discontentment can be quite subtle, and is often not perceived by the person as the underlying cause of their anxiety. If you do not understand the specific cause of your anxiety, look at any areas of your life you feel dissatisfied by.

We all have emotional and social needs. You can centre your inquiry around these pivotal areas:

- Safety and security
- Self-control and autonomy

- Competencies and accomplishment
- Intimacy and connection
- Personal meaning and value
- Belonging to a wider community
- Working with others towards a common goal

Whilst keeping these social and emotional needs in mind, ask yourself, "Is there something lacking in my life?"

Perhaps you don't feel safe at home? Perhaps you don't feel secure in your job? Maybe you are worried about your relationship breaking down? Maybe you don't feel in control of your life? Perhaps you feel a sense of unworthiness due to a lack of contact with community? Maybe you don't get enough privacy? Perhaps you don't feel like you're achieving much in life or being challenged in any meaningful way? Maybe you don't feel accepted or valued by people in your life?

Evaluate your needs and begin to identify any actions you can take that will make you feel more contented and satisfied. By being pro-active in seeking to address aspects of your life you feel discontented by, you will alleviate anxiety. This is because, when you take action to help yourself, you are discharging the stress response. And as you generate more contentment and satisfaction in life, you will likely overcome any generalised anxiety.

Sometimes, it can also help to ask yourself, "What would I be doing differently if I did not have anxiety?" Make a list of things you would like to be doing, that you feel anxiety is holding you back from. Then assess each of the items on your list and place them on a scale of how challenging they seem. Begin with the least challenging item, make plans to do it and then go and do it. The more you push through your fears, the more confidence you will gain, and this will alleviate anxiety.

Changing your thinking style so that you do not generate further negative emotions is also very important for overcoming anxiety. If a person spends an inordinate amount of time worrying and ruminating, this can cause or exacerbate stress and anxiety. Often, people over-dwell on the past or worry too much about the future. But ask yourself, "What can I do now, in this present moment?"

One solution, is simply to find ways to unwind from stress by doing things that get you out of the worry cycle. Maybe you could play an instrument, go for a walk, read, write, cook, draw, dance, watch a movie, meet a friend, go to a Tai Chi class, mow the lawn or play a sport. Any activity that gets you out of your own mind and focuses you on something outside of yourself can relieve you from worrying.

Mindfulness is a technique that can help keep you in the present moment and many people have experienced positive changes from practicing mindfulness, particularly, in overcoming anxiety.

To practice what is known as mindfulness, you essentially become an observer, without judgement or opinion. It can take some practice as most of us become conditioned to have opinions and judgements about pretty much everything. Try and sit on a bench on a busy high street or in a shopping mall on a Saturday afternoon. Can you remain in a state of non-judgement? Can you stop your mind from voicing its opinions? Or do you find there is a running commentary occurring in your mind such as, 'Wow, he's got a lot of shopping', 'Goodness, I would never wear that colour', 'She's really overweight', 'He's obviously rich', 'That kid looks so happy' etc.

When practicing mindfulness, if a thought occurs regarding what you're doing, what you're observing or any other concerns — then be aware of the thought, observe the thought, but try not to react to it, or start analysing or making up opinions about it. Over time, you can train yourself to not react and to simply observe. By doing this, you will be able to remain in an undisturbed present moment, with a calm mind, uncluttered by opinions and judgements.

It is our own attitudes, opinions and judgements that are often the primary source of our discontent and unease. And to alleviate anxiety you have to make an effort to neutralise thoughts and emotions that generate a friction within you. These are often the thoughts and emotions that come from reactions to situations or people in your life. Disappointment, indignation, jealousy, resentment, self-pitying and frustration are some common examples. If your inner dialogue becomes dominated by negative sentiments; stress will occur, and this can lead to anxiety.

Perhaps you blame and judge people in a way that offsets taking responsibility for your life. Whatever has happened in your life and whatever other people have done to you, it will be a detriment to yourself to keep blaming situations and people. If you blame, you will end up replaying thoughts and emotions that can then keep you stuck in an anxiety response. By accepting what happened and taking responsibility for your life, you take control. When you take control, you can be pro-active in moving forward, and this shift in attitude will alleviate anxiety.

Life can be difficult at times and people can sometimes act in ways that are very unsavoury. But you always have a choice about how you react. You can either accept what happened and perhaps take appropriate action to resolve the situation. Or you can get caught up in a downward spiral of negative thinking and emotional reacting that will then cause you stress and could lead to anxiety.

Another good technique for changing your attitude and thinking style, is to begin to challenge and replace negative thoughts, so that you are either neutralising them or replacing them with positive interpretations.

To start with, over the course of one week, make a note of all the negative thoughts and emotions that you have. Don't judge yourself or over-think this exercise, just write down all the negative thoughts and emotions you have over the course of one week. At the end of the week take a look at your list. Were the thoughts rational? Can you think of different interpretations? Were you making assumptions and jumping to conclusions? Were you thinking only about worst-case scenarios? Can you see the situation from another perspective? So, you begin to challenge the validity of your negative thoughts and emotions.

People with anxiety tend to interpret events over-personally and can have irrational beliefs about their performance in life. They may have thoughts and make statements like, "I'm no good at that, I tried and failed, so I won't ever be able to do it."

We all have occasions in life when things don't turn out as we hoped they would. To avoid creating a cycle of anxiety, it is important to accept these events, and to recognise that it is irrational to allow the thoughts and emotions we felt in the past, to be replayed over and over whenever a similar challenge appears in life. You have to stop identifying with your perceived inadequacies. So, you stop thinking and talking about your perceived failures. You stop rigidly defining yourself and what you are capable of, and you allow yourself room to change.

Perhaps your standards are too high and you berate yourself for imperfections — causing yourself unnecessary stress and anxiety. Maybe you failed your driving test three times, but that doesn't mean there is something wrong with you. Just because something didn't go as planned before, does not mean it will always happen this way.

Many people with anxiety think too often about catastrophic outcomes when there is really no need to. For example, if you think extreme thoughts such as, "My life will be ruined if I lose my job." You are setting yourself up for anxiety and you are also irrationally limiting your perspective. If you did lose the job, perhaps you'd find a better job, or perhaps in the time not working, you'd find an even more satisfying path you could take in life. By training yourself to see more positive perspectives, you neutralise negativity, and you can then cope with the inevitable uncertainties in life.

Once you change how you perceive yourself and the things that happen in your life, you will come into a thinking style that is more rational, neutral, and accepting of yourself, other people and your life circumstances. You won't unduly worry about potential outcomes as you will be able to trust that whatever happens, you'll be able to adapt. You won't have to counter negativity with positive interpretations, as your mind will be at ease. You will have proven to yourself through your resilience that you are strong, and when this happens, you will not suffer from the burden of unnecessary anxiety.

Focus on the good in yourself and your life, and recognise the strengths and resources you have. You can then generate and consolidate feelings of self-worth, gratitude and acceptance, and build a steady foundation from which to move forward.

Ensure you are well hydrated and eat a diet consisting mostly of natural non-processed foods. Monitor your caffeine intake from tea, coffee, fizzy drinks and chocolate. Sometimes, it can be as simple as drinking more clean water and eliminating caffeine from your diet to resolve anxiety. Also, monitor your sugar intake — too much sugar, especially refined white sugar, can cause mood fluctuations and anxiety.

Purge your body of excess stress hormones through regular movement and do some form of aerobic exercise that you enjoy at least two or three times a week. Also, if you have the opportunity, a simple five-minute exercise can be done whenever you feel stressed or shortly after. So, if you begin to feel anxious, jog on the spot for a few minutes. It may sound silly, but it works, as you will burn off the stress hormones and deactivate the fight or flight survival mechanism.

Learn how to relax using the methods I provided in the earlier chapter Relaxation Techniques. By regularly practicing relaxation techniques you can manage your stress levels and prevent anxiety from occurring. In particular, the method of breathing out for slightly longer than you breathe in is useful for overcoming anxiety.

When you are relaxed, stress responses become deactivated and arousal in your nervous system can be alleviated. If you have been experiencing anxiety for a long time, it can take some time for the arousal in your nervous system to dissipate. But if you persevere with relaxation techniques, you will notice positive changes.

It is also worth mentioning that certain medications can sometimes cause anxiety. If you are unsure of the source of your anxiety and are taking pharmaceuticals, do some research and inquire with your doctor. It is possible, you could alleviate anxiety by changing or stopping medication.

Overcoming a panic attack

A panic attack is a physiological reaction that can occur due to an overload of stress. They are usually over within a few minutes. A panic attack does not bare any physical or mental threat to a normal healthy person. The racing pulse and quickened breathing are being caused by the fight or flight mechanism and are components of the survival response.

A panic attack can cause an imbalance of oxygen intake and this can put a strain on chest muscles, leading to trembling and hyperventilation. These symptoms can lead to a sense of losing control, but you have to remember, if your health condition is normal, you are not at risk of dying. It is important that you do not fuel the panic by imagining and thinking irrationally about adverse scenarios.

Implement the breathing technique, whereby you breathe out for longer than you breathe in. This will counter the physiological effects being caused by the panic and will bring you into a more relaxed state. Some people like to count — 3 seconds breathing in, then 5 seconds breathing out and then at your own pace, increase the interval to 7 seconds breathing in and 11 seconds breathing out.

Step back from your thoughts and observe yourself. Notice your surroundings and your situation. Reassure yourself in as many ways as you can think of that you are safe. For example, you could reassure yourself that someone you trust is nearby, that you are not trapped, that you can breathe, and that you know what to do to calm your mind and relax your body. You can say in your mind, "With every breath, I am feeling calmer."

Although it may sound counter-intuitive, exercise can also assist a person to avoid a panic attack or even overcome one.

If you feel a panic attack coming on and you are healthy, try running up and down the stairs or round the block. In other words, take physical action to burn off the stress response.

CHAPTER TEN

Moving Beyond Trauma

The definition of trauma is twofold. It refers to a deeply distressing experience and also to the subsequent emotional shock. When a person continues to experience symptoms of emotional shock for a long period after a traumatic event, they are often diagnosed with Post Traumatic Stress Disorder (PTSD).

Recurring symptoms of trauma can include:

- Negative mood and beliefs. A sense of hopelessness, irritability, anxiety, depression.
- Guilt, blame, unworthiness, self-pity, self-destructive behaviours, loss of interest, introversion, distrust.
- Numbness, dissociation, derealisation (unreality of surroundings, feeling it's not real).
- Distressing dreams, memories, flashbacks, physiological reactions resembling the traumatic experience.
- A strong desire to avoid anything associated with the

trauma.

• Poor sleep, hypervigilance, easily startled, concentration issues, memory issues.

Psychologists usually deem a person to have PTSD if some of the above symptoms occur for more than a month after a distressing event.

PTSD is when the brain does not fully deactivate from the state of intense emotional arousal caused during a distressing experience. When someone has PTSD, their brain remains on high alert in anticipation of anything that may threaten their survival. Any stimuli picked up through the senses that resembles the traumatic experience instantly sets off physiological and psychological alert signals.

This alert system is a biologically evolved part of all humans and is enacted from the older part of the brain known as the limbic system. The amygdala is the organ within the limbic system that is responsible for instigating this alert system. This system is often referred to as the fight or flight survival mechanism.

Incoming information from the senses is scanned by the amygdala for potential threats and cross referenced with a record of survival related memories. Normally, this information is then passed on to the hippocampus, encoded as a sensory memory, before being passed to the neo-cortex. However, when stress is at a very high level; communication between these organs falters and priority is given to the amygdala and the fight or flight survival mechanism. Information relating to a traumatic event can therefore become trapped in the amygdala, resulting in excessive firing of the fight or flight survival mechanism.

The problems are exacerbated because the amygdala cannot distinguish between thought and sensory information. So, any thoughts, emotions, memories or dreams can trigger the response. And these responses can be triggered by any kind of associated stimuli. The amygdala has evolved to look for anything similar, even metaphorically similar, to a survival threat.

For example, a person who has been traumatised during a war, may be triggered by a door slamming in the wind as the amygdala rapidly associates the slamming sound with the sound of gunfire that is stored in the trauma imprint. A person who was traumatised by a life-threatening car accident, may be triggered by the colour red as the amygdala associates the colour with the red car they collided with. A person may have been traumatised through abuse by someone who wore a certain perfume or cologne and smelling that again can be a trigger.

If the trauma imprint is activated due to a trigger; sensory memories can become reloaded and experienced physiologically. For example, a person traumatised in a car accident may experience the taste of blood, the smell of petrol, feelings of pain, claustrophobia and panic. Thought memories can become reloaded also, inducing flashbacks and dissociations.

Trauma imprints can also become activated by subconscious triggers that are not perceived at the level of the conscious mind. A person can therefore find themselves in a state of physical and emotional shock, reliving trauma symptoms, for reasons they do not fully understand.

Managing Trauma Symptoms

If you are experiencing trauma symptoms, as a first priority, you should ensure you have a place where you can feel relatively safe. Ideally, you should get away from threatening places, situations and people that are connected with the cause of the trauma.

Trauma overstimulates the nervous system, meaning arousal levels can be chronically high. Frequently being in this state of alertness can cause irritability, anger, hypervigilance, fatigue and poor concentration. It is imperative for a person suffering with trauma symptoms to learn relaxation techniques. In particular, the breathing techniques and visualisation methods that I wrote about in the earlier chapter titled, Relaxation Techniques. Physical exercise can also be an effective way to discharge a heightened state of arousal.

A trigger is essentially a piece of information that reminds you of something that happened in the past. Identifying your triggers can be stressful, and should not be attempted until you have become proficient at inducing yourself into relaxation. It is worth the effort though, as by identifying triggers, you can process emotions associated with the trauma. You can become more adept at recognising that the triggers are simply reminders of the past and are not relevant to the present time. This process can help you to defuse and efficiently manage any re-activation of trauma symptoms.

Relaxation is fundamental to this process because if you are triggered, the fight or flight mechanism can become activated. And if this happens, access to your neo-cortex will be inhibited. It is our higher mind, the neo-cortex, that can rationally assess situations and confirm that there is not a threat in the present time. When you are calm and relaxed, you have access to your higher mind.

If you are confident that you can bring yourself into a relaxed state, begin to try and identify triggers and become aware of them. Make a note of what you were doing at the time they occurred. In particular, look to see if you can identify if there are sensory inputs that trigger you. Such as something you were looking at, hearing, touching, smelling or tasting. Also, can you identify any specific behaviours from other people that trigger you?

If there are certain places, objects or people that trigger you, and you can easily avoid them, then structure your life so that this is possible. Although, if these triggers are not in any way an actual threat to you, at some stage, it will be helpful to gradually expose yourself to them. You can then recognise them as reminders of your past, that are not in any way a threat to you now in the present.

You can also begin to rewire your associations by consciously creating new connections that are more neutral or inspiring. For example, if a certain colour triggers you, find something in this colour and create new memories by thinking about the colour in a different context. So, you can go through a process of diluting the strength of your triggers by inputting new memories and associations.

For example, if some trauma symptoms are triggered by the colour red, you could spend time focusing on red roses that you associate with a pleasant smell. So, if you then become triggered by the colour red, you can bring your attention to other associations you have, in this case, you would imagine red roses and their pleasant scent. This technique has its limitations, but is effective for certain triggers, especially ones that are more generalised, such as a colour, taste, smell or other sensory stimuli.

If you try and suppress intrusive memories, you can often end up feeling more threatened by them. This can then lead to a build-up of further apprehension and fear regarding the memories recurring. It is best to try and accept the memory has arisen and then limit your reaction by framing the memory in the past, taking measures to relax yourself and possibly thinking of other associations you may have that could defuse the trigger.

Becoming acutely aware of your surroundings can also be a helpful strategy to defuse triggers. You can make a conscious effort to notice the room you are in, the objects, the colours, the smells, the texture of the furniture you can feel with your hands. Identify different elements within your surroundings, and focus your attention and thoughts on them. All of this awareness helps to confirm that you are in a different and safe environment, and are not in the environment where the trauma occurred. It anchors you in the present moment and can therefore counter trauma symptoms.

Getting in touch with the sensations in your body can help to keep your attention in the present. The Body Scan relaxation technique provided in an earlier chapter is particularly helpful for this. Bring focused awareness to relaxing any parts of your body you experience discomfort or tension in.

Practicing movement exercises such as Chi Gong, Tai Chi or Yoga can also be greatly beneficial and can serve to discharge tension and emotion, and keep you grounded in your body. Some form of rhythmic movement may also help. For example, dancing, bouncing a ball, banging on a drum or simply allowing your body to rock or sway at a pace that feels soothing.

Shaking and trembling are sometimes experienced as trauma symptoms, and occur if a person freezes due to feeling helpless. It has been noted in animal research that animals who were chased by a predator and managed to escape, will shake and tremble for a period of time after the distress of being chased. Researchers postulate this is a mechanism developed to discharge their traumatic experience. Shaking and trembling are also noted to relieve humans of trauma symptoms and there are techniques designed to help facilitate this. One example is the modality known as Tension and Trauma Releasing Exercises (TRE). There are classes anyone can attend that are quite widely available.

Any type of self-care activity will be helpful to alleviate trauma symptoms. In particular, looking after your body and mind with good food, plenty of water, exercise and time in nature will be beneficial. Try to keep your home organised and free from unnecessary clutter. Make it a safe space. Remove any items that you associate with a threat to your safety. Place items that remind you of positive memories and sentiments in each room.

If you are suffering with hypervigilance, ensure you feel safe as often as possible. So, for example, when you're at home, make sure the doors are locked, and then confirm to yourself that you are in a safe space. Spending time in nature can also be very helpful. A place where you feel safe and can, for example, sit by a river, or on a hillside and just be in peace and observe.

Strategies to manage trauma symptoms should always reinforce a sense of safety. Anything, that informs your body and mind that the trauma was in the past and that you are now living beyond it and are safe, will be beneficial. As applicable, it can be helpful to remind yourself:

- That the traumatic event was in the past.
- How different and safe your current environment is.
- That people care about you and are contactable or close by.

- Your physical injuries have healed or are not life threatening anymore.
- That you are making progress.

To heal trauma, the imprint of traumatic information being held in the amygdala needs to be removed and recoded in the neo-cortex as a memory of the past. Thus, being fully recognised and processed by the brain and nervous system as not being imminently necessary for survival in the present.

In many cases, healing will take place over time if relaxation and other measures are taken to manage and defuse symptoms. Gradually, symptoms subside as the body and mind fully realise they can let go of the heightened level of alertness.

Coping Skills

Trauma can change the way a person perceives the world. Due to consistently feeling threatened and unsafe, a person can feel very vulnerable and low in mood. This can result in depression and anxiety, and the information provided in the previous two chapters can be applied to resolving these symptoms.

People with PTSD will often irrationally view the world through the lens of their trauma and then misjudge circumstances and other people. It is therefore helpful to challenge negative thinking, assumptions, self-depreciation, blame and self-pity. And to focus attention on your strengths and resources, whilst also making an effort to do activities you enjoy, and spend time socialising with people you trust.

People have varying coping styles when confronted with

challenging situations in life. These coping styles become particularly significant if a person is healing from a trauma. Psychologists have determined the following characteristics as being the most helpful:

- Open to discussing their feelings, sociable, seek assistance from others.
- Can understand and derive meaning from the trauma.
- Can draw personal strength from the challenge and work towards goals.
- Self-motivated and able to organise and structure their life in a manageable way.
- Confident in their ability to cope.
- Sense of humour and hope.

As appropriate, see if you can incorporate the above coping styles into your mental attitude to assist you further.

Self-destructive behaviours often occur when a person feels they cannot cope. It is an attempt to try and escape painful memories by numbing them out. For example, a person may turn to alcohol, drugs or self-harm. A couple of drinks or a marijuana joint can make some people feel better and more relaxed. But alcohol or drugs taken in excess, or to the point of long-term dependency, will be counter-productive and will not help their healing process.

Self-destructive behaviours are usually a displacement of emotion. If someone hurts themselves, it is often an expression of self-neglect that is rooted in discontentment and a lack of self-acceptance. Or it is a way of expressing emotions they feel about other people, yet they direct the emotions at themselves rather than at others. The solutions are, to learn coping skills and bravely face through the emotions so that they can be processed. Whilst also focusing on activities that engender self-care and self-respect. Professional assistance should be sought in all serious cases of self-destructive behaviour and self-harm.

Professional Treatments

Talking about a trauma can assist a person to release stored-up emotion, integrate the event into the past and contextualise the experience into a normal memory. However, many psychologists, counsellors and psychotherapists are not skilled in holding a safe space whilst keeping a person relaxed. The issue, is that by talking about the trauma, the trauma imprint is re-activated, and unless a person is able to deeply relax during this process, no integration can occur and the trauma imprint will often end up becoming further embedded.

This is why there has been some success with using substances such as methylene-dioxin-amphetamine (MDMA) and psilocybin when treating a person with PTSD. Due to the deep states of relaxation these compounds can induce, a person can go through a re-activation of their trauma, and be guided through a process of integration whilst remaining in a deeply relaxed state. Thus, bypassing the fight or flight survival mechanism and allowing the imprint to be removed from the amygdala.

If the trauma imprint is activated and a person can remain relaxed, the amygdala can finally accept there is no longer an imminent threat to survival, and can let the imprint go. Any process that can turn a traumatic memory into an ordinary memory can cure post-traumatic stress.

The techniques listed below have had some limited success, the first two are officially sanctioned for treatment of PTSD by many health authorities around the world:

- Eye Movement Desensitization Reprocessing (EMDR)
- Trauma Focused Cognitive Behavioural Therapy (TF-CBT) & Cognitive Processing Therapy (CPT)
- Emotional Freedom Technique (EFT otherwise known as Tapping)

EMDR and Tapping are thought to be effective for some people because the movement involved in the treatment enables attention to be focused away and dissociated from the emotional shock of the trauma. Thus, a person can talk about the traumatic experience, whilst remaining in a low state of emotional arousal — allowing the neocortex and hippocampus to work with the amygdala and create a new context for the trauma that changes its meaning. Therefore, the memory can be recoded appropriately.

TF-CBT and CPT are rooted in the concept of 'exposure therapy' which means that a person is gradually exposed to aspects of the traumatic experience, including associations, and is then helped by the therapist to reframe the way they think about the experience and any associations. However, spending too much time focusing on the past will be counter-productive. And when asking a person to recall their trauma, if they are not sufficiently relaxed, the trauma can become more deeply embedded — the amygdala will still believe there is an imminent threat in the present. TF-CBT and CPT treatments for trauma are often unsuccessful.

Lesser known techniques that use guided imagery practices have been shown to have some success treating traumatic stress. A method known as the 'Visual Kinaesthetic Dissociation Technique' has shown some positive results, and also a similar method known as the 'Rewind Technique' has been shown to be a relatively reliable treatment for PTSD.

The Human Givens Institute have developed a version of the Rewind Technique and do have a successful track record of helping people resolve trauma symptoms. They assert, their version of the Rewind Technique can safely remove a trauma imprint from the amygdala, thus allowing the brain to process and reframe the memories as being no longer an active threat. This is achieved through activating the trauma template with exposure, guiding the person into a deeply relaxed state, using guided imagery to create a dissociation; that is then taken advantage of to indirectly view the traumatic memories in a forwards and backwards way, until there is no trace of emotional arousal.

The Rewind Technique is regarded to be effective at relieving people of trauma symptoms. But it can cause a short-term sense of derealisation, and detract a person from their natural coping and processing functions. This is definitely a worthwhile trade off if a person is being seriously afflicted. But people with mild symptoms of trauma can resolve their issues by learning ways to manage and defuse their symptoms — allowing their body and mind to naturally process and let go of the trauma.

It should also be noted that certain trauma treatments, such as the Rewind Technique, can also be applied to curing phobias and other conditions such as obsessive-compulsive disorders. Many psychological imbalances have their root in a traumatic experience.

Therapeutic Writing

Writing about your traumatic experience can be a therapeutic way of processing the memories and integrating them into the past. It is a form of exposure therapy and before proceeding you must feel confident that you can bring yourself into a relaxed state should you need to. Inevitably, some emotions and trauma symptoms are going to arise during this process. Without professional supervision, I only recommend this method for those who are experiencing mild trauma symptoms. If, at any time, you begin to feel overwhelmed then stop the process and begin to relax yourself.

Ensure you have a sufficient amount of time set aside and that you don't have to rush off to do anything major afterwards. Write in a place where you feel safe. Take your time, this does not need to be done quickly or in one session. You should be sure to always write about your experiences in the past tense.

• Firstly, write down a timeline of the events that occurred from a bird's eye view. So, you are just reporting like a journalist what happened, without reporting your own thoughts, sensations and feelings that occurred. If you don't remember exactly what happened, then write down what you do remember or what you know to be true.

• Then write down what happened from your perspective. How you felt, what you saw, heard, smelt, tasted etc. Take your time and remember to stop if you feel the need to calm yourself and relax. It is often best to write about the least traumatic aspects of the experience first. Don't worry about writing in chronological order.

• As a separate exercise, write about your healing journey and the progress you have made. You can also write about your hopes and aspirations. Note all that you are grateful for.

Peak Experiences

Trauma can change a person's neural pathways in detrimental ways. And recurring trauma symptoms often then reinforce these neural pathways, and prolong the anguish. On the flip side, profoundly positive experiences can also change neural pathways and lead to positive changes. Examples include, profound states of ecstasy, rapture, bliss and joy. In psychology, these experiences are often referred to as *peak experiences*. Peak experiences can over-write detrimental neural pathways and lead a person to experience a positive and healing transformation.

With regard to healing imbalances caused by stress and trauma, peak experiences are known to be very effective. Yet, due to the personal nature of these experiences, a reliable formula to re-create them for people has proven to be somewhat elusive. Peak experiences are more likely to occur:

• When a person is calm and in the present moment.
• When they have reached a state of acceptance about the traumatic event.
• When they have faced the implications of the trauma with courage and have persevered with their healing process.

What can then happen, is a person experiences some form of profound epiphany whereby a new perspective becomes apparent. They often perceive profound meaning and purpose relating to the traumatic experience, along with an understanding about how to move forward and transform the traumatic experience into something positive. This sometimes involves the motivation to assist others who have gone through similar traumatic experiences.

If a peak experience happens to you, take time to embody it and assimilate it by reflecting on your new perspectives and feelings. You should also take actions that affirm the transformation as soon as possible. This will reinforce the neural pathways that have been changed.

The type of peak experiences that are most effective at healing trauma often have a deeply philosophical or spiritual nature. These experiences can happen spontaneously, but are usually the result of a sustained effort to heal oneself that culminates in a deeply humbling and sometimes mystical experience. Meditation is one example known to enhance the potential of a peak experience.

CHAPTER ELEVEN

Nutrition For Your Mind

Everyone is slightly different, and when it comes to diet, you have to follow what works for you. But there are certain recommendations for optimising the health of your brain and nervous system. And research suggests the following tips can have a significantly positive effect on psychological well-being.

A balanced level of glucose:
- Dark green, leafy vegetables and root vegetables are most recommended. Notable mentions are sweet potatoes, cauliflower, Brussel sprouts, carrots, arugula and beetroot. It is best to not overcook vegetables — steaming or cooking slowly on a low heat will provide more nutrients.
- Fresh fruit such as melon and blueberries. But limit fruits high in glucose such as bananas unless eating after exercise.
- Oats and gluten-free grains.

- Mostly avoid refined sugar, including sucrose. A limited intake of honey, maple syrup or coconut sugar is recommended.
- Mostly avoid overly processed and refined foods.

Essential fats and proteins:
- Seeds such as flax, pumpkin, chia, sesame and hemp seeds are high in essential fats and protein. To aid digestion, you can blend seeds in a smoothie or you can ground them and take a tablespoon each day. Cold-pressed seed oils are also recommended.
- Nuts contain a lot of essential fats and protein. They are easier to digest after being soaked, some people like to dehydrate them after soaking.
- Wild fish twice a week. Oily fish such as mackerel, herring, anchovy, sardines, trout or salmon are best. If you buy farmed fish, try to ensure it is farmed organically. Fish oil supplements such as Arctic krill oil are an option.
- Free range organic meats and bone broth are a good source of essential fats and proteins. But it's not recommended to eat meat too often. You can experiment with eating different amounts. For example, some people find eating meat once a week is a good balance for them.
- Beans, lentils, peas or chick peas eaten with rice or quinoa.
- Avocado.
- Eggs. Free range and organic when possible.
- Organic butter, ghee and coconut oil. Mostly avoid foods cooked with hydrogenated 'vegetable' oils.
- Primrose oil supplement.

Vitamins and minerals either from food or supplements:
(see the Notes section for corresponding foods)
- All B vitamins
- Folic acid
- Magnesium
- Manganese
- Zinc
- Beta-carotene
- Vitamin C
- Vitamin E
- Co-enzyme Q
- Chromium
- Tryptophan (available in many foods, see list in Notes section)
- Iodine (best from food sources such as kelp, seaweeds, fish)

You can take specific herbal remedies or supplements to boost memory, mood and motivation:
- Ashwagandha
- Gotu Kola
- Ginkgo biloba
- Rosemary
- Resveratrol
- L-Theanine
- 5-HTP (not recommended if you are taking psychiatric medication)
- N-Acetyl-L-Cysteine (NAC)
- Cannabidiol (CBD)
- Alpha Lipoic Acid (ALA)
- Choline
- L-glutamine

- L-tyrosine
- Methylmethionine (Vitamin U)
- Rhodiola (Rhodiola rosea) plant

You can take certain foods to assist with relaxation:
- Kava Kava
- Valerian
- Holy basil leaf
- Passion flower
- Lavender
- Chamomile
- Cacao (does contain caffeine that can cause anxiety in some people)

Further Advice

- The microbiome in your gut effects mood regulation, memory and cognition. Indigestion can cause mental unease. Ensure the bacteria in your microbiome is living symbiotically by getting a balance of healthy bacteria from your diet. Raw fruits and vegetables are valuable sources. Also, sauerkraut, kombucha, miso, natto, fermented milk, kefir and yogurt are rich in healthy bacteria, digestive enzymes and probiotics. To resolve digestive imbalances, you could supplement with a course of L-glutamine, zinc, magnesium, omega-3 fish oils and probiotic capsules. Reishi, Cordyceps and Lion's Maine mushroom supplements can be highly beneficial as well.
- The most common foods linked to mental imbalances are gluten and dairy products. Remove gluten and dairy from your diet for a period of time if any mental imbalances occur.

- Excess inflammation in the body has been linked to fatigue, fogginess and mental imbalances. You can prevent excess inflammation by avoiding overly processed foods, limiting deep fried foods, eating smaller meals, drinking more water and exercising regularly. Gluten products in particular can cause excessive inflammation. Also, nightshade vegetables can cause excess inflammation for some people. Examples include: Tomatoes, peppers, potatoes, aubergine (eggplant), courgette (zucchini). You can decrease inflammation with antioxidant rich foods — berries are particularly effective, also pineapple, turmeric, ginger and Brazil nuts.

- Artificial ingredients such as man-made sweeteners, food additives and E numbers can cause unnatural mental stimulation. Some people are also susceptible to mood swings caused by caffeine from tea, coffee, colas or chocolate.

- Metal poisoning from lead, cadmium, mercury, aluminium and excess copper has been linked to mental imbalances. If you realise you are burdened by metal poisoning, I suggest you connect with a detox specialist, clinical nutritionist or naturopathic doctor to get advice on detoxing your body.

- Research suggests, without enough vitamin B3 (niacin), B6, folic acid and B12; your brain cannot maintain a healthy balance of neurotransmitters such as dopamine and serotonin.

- Many people diagnosed with schizophrenia have been cured with high doses of vitamin B3, B12 and folic acid, whilst also supplementing at normal levels with zinc and B6. People with anxiety are also helped in particular by vitamin B3. People with depression are helped greatly by foods high in tryptophan, B vitamins and omegas 3 and 6.

- Your thoughts and emotions effectively act like nutrients and can affect your body and mind. Try not to eat when you are stressed as the food will often not be properly digested. By maintaining calmness, you will aid digestion, nutritional absorption, and positively affect your neurochemistry.

- It is good to acknowledge the psychological benefits of eating foods we simply enjoy and to not become too rigid about a 'healthy' diet. If a person fears a certain food yet eats it, this can then lead them to experience indigestion. Our bodies can cope fine in moderation with processed, high in sugar, completely 'unhealthy' foods.

- It is fine to enjoy some occasional indulgences and just don't worry about it. But remember to monitor how you feel after eating different foods. This will give you the information required to make wise choices. For example, a chocolate cake may feel really good at the time and boost your mood. But then you may feel a slump in mood and energy two hours later. Was it worth it? Maybe it totally was! But it probably isn't going to work for you to do it every afternoon.

Supplementation

It is recommended to get vitamins and minerals from food sources. But if you intend to use supplements as part of a healing program to resolve certain imbalances, they can provide a beneficial boost to get you back on track.

It is usually best to consult with a naturopath or nutritionist who can advise you more specifically for your needs. Unless you have consulted with a health professional who provides specific instructions — you should always take the recommended dosage as instructed on the label.

CHAPTER TWELVE

Believing in Yourself

From the day we are born until around age seven, our brains are mostly in a trance state and are primed to absorb information. We assimilate, store and organise this information into an archive of pattern matches and associations from which meaning is inferred. Through this meaning, we develop beliefs. From around age seven, the conscious mind is formed and we are more able to choose and direct the meaning we infer from our own experiences, and thus begin to form our own individual beliefs. However, by this stage, people have usually already assimilated many limiting beliefs about themselves and their world.

As children, we are very susceptible to the beliefs of adults and older children, and are greatly influenced by them. We imitate behaviours and we internalise beliefs. We are also subjected to many judgements and many rules that contribute to the formation of our early belief patterns.

Children will often develop beliefs about themselves based

on how they interpret the way they are treated. If they are ignored, they can infer this to mean that what they have to say is not important. If they do not get what they want, they can infer this to mean that they are not worthy. If they are punished, they can infer this to mean that they are not accepted and that they are a 'bad' person.

If these interpretations continue and the child does not perceive alternative interpretations; the inferences of meaning can then become internalised as self-beliefs. And as a child develops a conscious mind, they can begin to identify with these beliefs. These beliefs can then form part of the personality that develops.

For example, if a child fails a math exam, the experience of 'failure' can be interpreted by the child to mean that they are not competent at math. This can then be internalised as a belief, leading the child to lose motivation to continue learning math and to resign themselves to being, 'bad at math'. This predicament would then be compounded if a parent or teacher continued to reinforce this belief. As opposed to providing encouragement, support, and the opportunity for the child to infer new interpretation and meaning.

As life goes on, a repository of experience and meaning continues to be assimilated. People form beliefs about themselves by observing their own thoughts, feelings, behaviours and experiences. Whilst, on top of this, they also form beliefs about themselves based on other people's reactions to them. People then make generalisations about their personality and their abilities based on beliefs that have formed.

Yet, beliefs are often formed from a hotchpotch of opinions, assumptions, judgements, inferences and convictions. Beliefs are not necessarily supported by evidence, are not necessarily rational, and are not necessarily applicable for the long term. Beliefs are interpretations of meaning and perception. They are not necessarily true.

What tends to happen, is the mind looks for patterns of meaning that it can associate with it's archive of past experiences. When a pattern match occurs, this can provide added weight and support for a belief. For example, if a person believes they are incompetent at math, this belief will restrict them, but it will also prime them to find confirmation for this belief. So, when an occasion arises and math is necessary, their mind will become discombobulated by their belief that they are incompetent at math, and they will likely make an error. This error can then be interpreted as further evidence to reinforce their belief that they are 'bad at math'. And thus, the belief becomes stronger.

When a person is placed under hypnosis, they can be led to believe that an elephant is standing in the room in front of them and they will see and hear an elephant standing in front of them. This is the power of belief — it can be so strong that it can actually affect our perception of reality.

To a lesser extreme, we are all being subjected to suggestion in our daily lives. Advertisements that employ psychological research to market products to people in the media are one example. But we are also influenced by what other people say and do, in particular, those people we respect as authority figures. This can lead to *introjections* — whereby we unconsciously adopt the ideas or attitudes of others and internalise them as beliefs. You do, at times, have to question why you have certain beliefs, because there is a chance they are in fact someone else's beliefs that you have unconsciously assimilated.

Many of our beliefs lurk in the far reaches of our subconscious and were placed there during our childhood.

For example, if you were repeatedly told by your parents that you would catch a cold if you got wet in the rain, then you may have internalised this as a belief. This belief would therefore make it more likely you would develop a cold if you got wet in the rain. Regardless of whether you recall your parents saying this, the belief in the subconscious can become initiated if a pattern match is detected. This pattern matching system has access to all your memories, including those you cannot normally recall that are stored in your subconscious. Pattern matches are often formed from cause and effect corollaries. In this example of a belief pattern, getting wet in the rain is the *cause* and a runny nose and a cold is the *effect*.

The power of suggestion given by medical professionals is well documented. Placebo sugar pills have been given to patients who were told the pills would cure them of their illness. On thousands of occasions, the belief instigated by the doctor, led to miraculous recoveries. Fake operations have also been used. For example, arthritis patients were told they were receiving an operation to cure their condition, yet in fact, they only received a scalpel scar and no operation took place. Many of these patients no longer suffered with arthritis pain. The corollary in this instance, is that the medical intervention was believed by the patients to be the cause and the effect was healing. But the placebo effect demonstrates that belief alone is powerful enough to initiate the healing in many cases. In other words, even if the cause is not real or what the person perceives, the effects can still occur if the belief in the cause is strong.

Our primary source of suggestion is our own mind. Through our thoughts and the words we utter, we make suggestions to ourselves. And this is, in many regards, a form of self-hypnosis and it can be very influential. For example, people who obsessively believe they are overweight will often see a distorted reflection in the mirror — they will actually see themselves differently than what is real. This is an example that is profound because it reveals how our beliefs can even warp our perceptions of our own physical form. Yet, this is really no different to holding a firm belief, such as being incompetent at math. In both cases, the belief can be strong enough to distort and limit the perception of what is real and what is possible.

People often have irrational beliefs, in particular, about themselves. Yet, many of their beliefs are based on evidence they have not challenged. It is often a worthwhile process to identify our beliefs and to trace back the reasoning for those beliefs.

You can try this exercise. Write down five core beliefs you have about yourself. Then go through each belief and attempt to go back in time and determine how and why these beliefs were formed. Look to see if you can recognise the roots of the beliefs and how these beliefs were then reinforced by subsequent experiences. Then assess whether these beliefs are completely rational. Are they based on solid evidence? Are they truly your own beliefs or are they someone else's?

In particular, any beliefs we have about ourselves that are limiting, are worth challenging. Look to identify the things that you tell yourself, *I can't do* or *I'm not good at*. Then attempt to trace back the roots of these beliefs, and challenge them. Why can't you do it? Why do you belief you are not good at it? Are your answers rational? Could you perhaps change these beliefs? Are they really set in stone?

Also, look for any cause and effect corollaries you may have wrapped up in your belief patterns. Often, our belief patterns can become rather rigid equations. So, you may believe that you can't do something until you've done something else. For example, perhaps you believe you are not worthy of a relationship until you get a highly paid job. But by holding this belief pattern, you are restricting yourself from entering what could be a perfect relationship for you. Challenge any belief equations you have, as maybe, they are completely erroneous.

People tend to have some specific fears and negative self-beliefs. In many cases, our fears develop as a way of protecting ourselves. For example, perhaps as a child you were ridiculed when you spoke up in class and so you developed a fear of public speaking because you wanted to protect yourself from being rejected. Or maybe you have a subconscious fear about becoming wealthy because your parents resented wealthy people. So, you internalised their beliefs and the meaning you inferred impacted your aspirations for wealth — because you didn't want your parents to resent you. But even belief patterns that are held deep in your subconscious can be changed.

Your self-concept is mostly constructed by how you perceive yourself based on your beliefs. What you perceive you are, is what you believe you are. But you can change your beliefs. You can unlearn what you have learned. You can recompose your core beliefs about yourself and change. You can let go of who you think you are and allow yourself to change. Think back over your life and remember how many beliefs you've had that have already changed. Changing beliefs is a natural process and you can consciously instigate this process.

Many of your beliefs are rooted in your subconscious mind. You will need to change your thoughts, speech, feelings and actions in order to interrupt the subconscious patterns. You have to be willing to commit to the changes you want. And you will have to push through some resistance, especially when changing some of your core belief patterns.

Firstly, identify any limiting self-beliefs that you can easily discard. Get rid of them. Any labels or characterisations you have about yourself that are limiting or derogatory — discard them. Stop identifying with categorisations and generalisations. Ditch as many 'I am...' statements as you can, in particular, any negative statements such as, 'I am poor', 'I am lonely', 'I am a shy person', 'I am bad at this'. If you want to change, then you have to stop identifying with the past. You have to stop reinforcing old beliefs that are holding you back.

Monitor your inner dialogue and your speech closely. If you notice yourself making statements such as, 'I can never get this right' or 'I always mess this up' or 'I don't believe I can do it', then counter these statements so that you recondition your belief patterns in a more empowering way. For example, *'I can get this right and I will persist until I do'*. So, you change your thoughts and your speech in a way so they become consistent with the belief patterns that you want to have.

But you can't simply think and talk your way into new belief patterns, as your subconscious is also linked with your feelings. The fastest way to align your conscious mind with your subconscious mind is to take actions that provide evidence for a belief. Then you can begin to reprogram your beliefs by providing real world evidence. And from this evidence, new inferences of meaning can form new beliefs, and these will be reinforced by positive emotions and feelings.

For example, if you think you are an incompetent public speaker, and you want to develop a belief that you are a competent public speaker, then you will have to actually go and do some public speaking and become more competent.

Only then can you consolidate the new belief by providing contrary evidence to break the old belief. Stretching yourself with challenges is the key to changing belief patterns.

In the process of changing beliefs, there will often be a period of inner conflict due to two opposing belief patterns being held simultaneously. Your consciousness is in the process of deciding which one is true, and so you have to keep pushing and providing evidence until one belief becomes dominant, then the dissonance will subside. When you take action and stick to your commitments, you will start to recondition your belief patterns. But you will often have to persevere and be disciplined.

For example, it is possible, that your first attempt at public speaking may not go as well as you hoped. But if you focus negatively on your performance and give into your initial fears and apprehensions, you will collapse back into your old belief patterns. You will then not cope as well with future public speaking opportunities. You avoid this by recognising your capabilities and what you are doing well. Give yourself credit for your efforts and focus on your strengths. Learn from your experiences and make changes as appropriate in order to improve and develop yourself. Don't worry about perfection. If you prove to yourself that you are resilient — that you are willing to keep moving forward whilst developing and challenging yourself — you will soon cross the threshold and form empowering and positive beliefs about yourself.

Another way to change your belief patterns is through mental rehearsal and visualisation. By practicing visualising yourself doing something in a confident and capable way, you will begin to change your neural pathways and will prime your brain to seek confirmation of these belief patterns. For example, if you mentally rehearse and visualise yourself making an excellent public speech, this will assist you to reinforce the belief pattern that you are an excellent public speaker.

As you begin to make changes, you may have to tell certain people in your life that you're changing. People often have a tendency to project onto us their limited perception of who they think we are — and their expectations and assumptions can be quite stifling if they do not give us room to change. If people in your life continue to denigrate you with projections, labels and generalisations, then limit your time with them. Begin to surround yourself with people who believe in your abilities, and can perceive the changes you are making. They will help to affirm and reinforce the beliefs you have about yourself and also the beliefs you are working to fortify in yourself.

When you are deciding what beliefs you want to instill and what beliefs you want to change — think about what is important to you. Think about the motivation for you wanting certain beliefs; and identify what the benefits of you having certain beliefs about yourself will be. What could you achieve if you held certain beliefs? Will you be held back from reaching your potential by your existing beliefs if you do not make changes?

Be patient when developing your beliefs. Some beliefs will change quickly, but others you will have to work at. Take responsibility for your beliefs and focus on making the beliefs you have about yourself empowering. Take action and find ways to fortify and enhance these beliefs. Persevere and keep on gathering evidence in support for your beliefs.

And remember, you don't need to have that many self-beliefs. It's better to have a handful of super-charged beliefs than a sack full of half-hearted beliefs. Much of the time, we only need to clear away our limiting beliefs, and then simply believe that we are capable of making progress in whatever we put our attention on.

Everyone is capable of fulfilling their potential, but they have to believe they are capable of fulfilling their potential. When you've made a concerted effort to consolidate empowering beliefs, you will find that your confidence and self-esteem will improve. You will feel more able to adapt to, learn from and negotiate the challenges of life. You will develop a faith in yourself — a self-assuredness.

Self Acceptance

The term *self-esteem* refers to the confidence a person has about their own value and ability. This confidence is built upon what a person deems their strengths and qualities to be, and is dismantled by what they deem their weaknesses and inadequacies to be. Levels of self-esteem fluctuate depending on how a person interprets their performance in life.

If a person becomes overly focused on their perceived weaknesses and inadequacies, this can lead to a low sense of self-esteem. This negative self-judgement can turn into a cycle of self-torment whereby a person routinely slips into self-depreciation, self-punishment and self-criticism. They will often feel inferior, embarrassed and ashamed. This can then lead to a sense of despair, hopelessness and cynicism — to the point where a person may decide that they deserve negativity in their life, because they are not worthy of anything else. Consistent self-criticism can even trigger a physiological stress response, and this can lead to mental and physical imbalances. The key to avoiding this is self-acceptance.

To accept yourself, you have to go through a process of self-reconciliation, whereby you make peace with yourself. You do this by accepting every facet of yourself, even the aspects of yourself you would rather not admit — you have to bring them into the light, acknowledge them and accept them as parts of yourself.

People are often afraid to fully accept themselves because they fear the consequences of their perceived weaknesses or inadequacies. This is usually due to fears of punishment or disapproval from the people in their lives or from society in general. Self-acceptance is often particularly difficult for people who have been indoctrinated by rigid religious concepts. For example, the concept of 'original sin' essentially dictates that each of us has a long list of things that are inherently wrong with us.

If a person believes there are parts of themselves that are 'wrong' they will find it hard to attain the inner peace of self-acceptance. And they may experience inner conflict if they are actively suppressing or denying what they believe about themselves to be wrong. This can lead to feelings of discontent, frustration, guilt and shame.

What tends to happen, is people reject parts of themselves because they believe these parts are not beneficial to their life. They believe that to get their needs met, they have to be a certain way. But if they struggle to adhere to these expectations they can end up struggling to accept themselves.

There are usually multiple layers underlying a lack of self-acceptance, and invariably these layers are linked to a person's desires to get their needs met. For example, if a person struggles to accept their body, this may result in them feeling unworthy of having an intimate relationship. If someone struggles to accept their current level of competency, they may be afraid their progress and security will be jeopardised. Yet, these acts of contrition lead to further self-esteem issues, and often result in the very thing being feared, being more likely to manifest. This is because the inner contrition leads to a reduction in confidence, and this can then lead a person to believe their opportunities are limited, and to change their behaviour based on these beliefs.

You can try this exercise. Consider any aspects of yourself that you do not feel comfortable with. At your own pace, bring each of these aspects under the spotlight. What is it about each aspect that you don't want to accept? What stops you from accepting these parts of yourself? What would happen if you could accept all of these aspects?

See if you can come to a place of closure with yourself by accepting these aspects. Allow yourself to feel any emotions that arise during this process. And try and unpack any information contained in the emotions, so that you can learn about yourself. Look to see if you can identify any desires that you might be restricting yourself from receiving due to inner contrition. Your intention here is to reintegrate aspects of yourself that may have become separated, and also to eradicate any lingering causes of self-criticism and self-depreciation.

Some of the aspects you identified, you may sincerely want to change as part of your development in life. It is healthy to have desires for personal change. But you can't easily change these parts of yourself if you cannot accept them. By accepting them, you step beyond the hindrances of inner struggle and conflict, and you reach a point of neutrality. From this neutral foundation you can then look at these aspects and either accept they are a natural part of yourself or you can work to transform them.

You accept yourself by ceasing to judge yourself. So, you

limit any assessments you have about yourself that are derogatory. You stop depreciating yourself. You no longer define aspects you deem to be inadequate, as being wrong. You no longer identify with any perceived inadequacies as being permanent features of yourself. You realise that any definitions you have about yourself are interpretations that can be changed. You re-evaluate the expectations you have for yourself and you throw out anything that is not rational or relevant. You treat yourself with compassion and respect. You change the way that you think and speak about yourself. No more statements such as, "I'm hopeless" or "I'm terrible at this."

Once you stop giving yourself a hard time and accept yourself, then you can restore your confidence. Freeing yourself from the hindrance of self-depreciation allows you to experience inner composure and peace.

You also have to come to terms with the decisions you have made in life. When you continue to regret things you've done, you are refusing to accept yourself. If you are languishing in regrets then these ruminations will create a sense of insecurity.

Make a list of any statements you regularly have floating around your mind that begin with:

- I should have…
- I could have…
- What if I'd…
- I wish I had…
- If only I'd not…

Can you accept what happened? What do you need to happen in order for you to let this go and accept the choices you made? Perhaps there is some action you can take to redeem yourself or maybe you can just let it go?

Try to identify the underlying reasons for your regrets and look at which of your needs are involved. For example, you may regret leaving a particular job ten years ago. But what exactly is it you think you have missed out on? What do you think you lost? Maybe you believe if you'd stayed in that job you would now have more money, more autonomy, more meaning, be more accomplished or have better friends. But make sure you question these assumptions rationally. Would this really be the case? And look at all the positive things that have happened because of the decisions you made. Was it really all that bad?

Look to identify the reasons for the decisions you made. What you will likely find is that you were doing your best with the information and level of understanding that you had at that time. If you still feel that you really did make a mistake, then make an effort to forgive yourself and let it go. You can't change the past. All you can do is recognise what you can learn from your experiences; and choose to either let things be or to take action to rectify the situation. So, you could identify what you feel you missed out on, and if you still want it, then you can take action that moves you towards it. You can neutralise any regrets you have via self-acceptance, self-forgiveness, reasoning and by taking action.

Once you begin a process of self-acceptance, you embark on a voyage of self-reconciliation. By recognising how you've been holding yourself back through self-depreciation and regret, you can make peace with yourself and take steps to move forward. The way forward is to embrace yourself with acceptance and compassion.

Self Compassion

You develop self-compassion by nurturing yourself and being kind to yourself. You become your biggest fan and you look after yourself. You invest time in yourself because you care. You focus on encouraging yourself by recognising and appreciating all of your strengths and successes. You build a positive rapport with yourself by reflecting on what you like about yourself, what you've achieved in life and what your potentials are.

Holding positive beliefs about yourself and caring compassionately about yourself will generate positive feelings. When you allow yourself to have positive beliefs about yourself, you will feel more peaceful, hopeful and content. Your self-esteem will rise due to the acceptance, respect and compassion you have for yourself.

If you are prone to self-depreciation, ensure that you put at least twice the effort and time into thinking about yourself in positive ways as opposed to negative ways. Over time, your efforts to counter any self-depreciation will become embedded as positive beliefs. When this occurs, less and less effort will be required, as your mind will enter more of a neutral state, and will not be prone to self-depreciating thoughts.

Self-pity can be healthy to a certain extent. It can bring you into a state of recognition of your suffering. But if you identify with your suffering and dwell in self-pity then you will enter into a state of victimhood. If you begin to enter into any self-pity, redirect the feelings into self-compassion whereby you focus on accepting and nurturing yourself. Then look to identify if there is anything you can do to help yourself and change your situation.

Whatever happens in life, if you can remain respectful and

tolerant of yourself, you will be able to grow and develop with ease. Any perceived failures and inadequacies can become lessons for growth in the journey of life. And with your self-esteem intact, you can continue your quest in life without being hindered and held back by unnecessary self-criticism.

You can try this exercise by answering these questions:

- What do I value about myself?
- How do I look after my body?
- How do I take care of myself mentally and emotionally?

Look through your answers and assess the levels of respect and compassion you have for yourself. Maybe you could think of ways you could further nurture your body and mind, and care for yourself with more compassion. Perhaps you could reflect on your strengths and resources more often and build your self-esteem.

The more you focus on your strengths and the more you nurture your body and mind — the more confidence you will attain. When you are confident and self-assured; self-depreciative thoughts and self-destructive behaviours will become a thing of the past.

Affirmations

Affirmations are statements consisting of words and phrases that reflect what you want to change or reinforce in your life. By repeating them, they can help to rewire neural pathways and change your beliefs, emotions and habits. You can design affirmations to specifically reinforce the changes you want to make to yourself and to your life.

To be most effective, affirmations should be repeated until

they become embedded in your mind, and you start to believe them. However, you also have to be taking some action in life to verify your beliefs — affirmations alone will not be enough.

You do have to remember, that certain affirmations may remind you about your fears or limiting beliefs. This can be counter-productive if you are not at the stage of also taking actions that reinforce and provide evidence for your affirmations. For example, you could bolster your belief in your public speaking abilities by affirming, "As I talk in public, I am calm and confident." But this example would be best to use once you actually have some experience with public speaking and are in the process of developing your practice. Before this time, you could work with a broader affirmation, such as, "With each new day, I am becoming a more confident person."

It is most effective to use the present tense when formulating affirmations. And also, you have to assess what particular words mean to you. What definitions in your mind do you hold for a word? What associations do you have with a word? For example, your associations with the word *wealth* may be more related to comfort and prosperity rather than money and affluence. Be clear about what you want, and use words that have the appropriate meaning to you.

You have to appreciate that your mind will know the truth of your situation and you have to also factor in that your mind has been conditioned to think in logical steps. So, as an example, if you wanted to create an affirmation for gaining wealth, instead of saying, "I am wealthy" you would say "With each new day I receive abundantly." If you wanted to affirm good health, instead of saying, "I am healthy" you would say, "In every moment, I am becoming healthier."

At first, your mind may persist in taunting you with doubt ridden thoughts and questions about your affirmations. Try not to react to any negative thoughts you may have about your affirmations and simply persevere. As long as your affirmations are aligned with your goals in life, and you are actually directing your focus and acting towards them, then the negative thoughts will fade and your affirmations will become your dominant beliefs. At which point, you will not have to keep repeating them, as they will be ingrained and internalised as your beliefs.

Here are some examples to give you some ideas. You can alter these phrases or add to them for your needs:

• My mind is calm and my body is strong.
• I feel at peace, I am composed and calm.
• I move through this day with power and strength.
• Whatever happens this day is beneficial for my evolution.
• By believing in my own strengths, I manifest what I desire.
• I am moving beyond limitations and I embrace positive change.
• As I continue to value myself, I become worthy of my needs.
• In every moment, I am able to love and accept myself.
• In every moment, my body is healing.
• With each new day all of my needs are being met.
• Today, I imbue kindness and respect, and I am open to receiving kindness and respect.
• With every step I take, I attract abundance into my life.
• I am always in the right place at the right time.
• With each new day I am becoming more peaceful.
• By focusing on my life, I am in control of my destiny.
• With each breath I take, I feel more and more relaxed.

- On this day I express the full potential within me.
- By expressing myself authentically, I am becoming free.
- By challenging myself I continue to grow.
- May the force within me energise my body and invigorate my mind.
- With courage I am stepping beyond my fears.
- I see the beauty in every person I meet.
- Through patience and dedication, I achieve all that I desire.
- By having faith and trust in myself, I fulfill my greatest potential.
- I am developing naturally as I learn and grow through experience.
- Because I am powerful my potential is boundless.

To make your own affirmations, start by thinking about your self-beliefs and how you perceive your life. What do you want to change? What are you working towards? What do you want to reinforce and fortify within yourself?

I suggest you formulate four affirmations for yourself. Keep the statements quite short and succinct. They can be specific or broad in their meaning. Write them down or print them out, and place them in places around your home where you'll notice them every day. Then take four minutes early in the morning and four minutes shortly before you go to bed to repeat your affirmations. You can repeat one affirmation for one minute and then move on to the next affirmation for one minute and so on. Stating your affirmations out loud can amplify their effectiveness, but saying them silently in your mind will also work.

It is often a good idea to develop some affirmations that are designed to keep you on track and reinvigorate you. If you feel off balance during the day, you can take a moment to relax and state your affirmations. As you continue to work with affirmations, you can choose to reduce your affirmations to single words.

It is also important to affirm the positive experiences you have in life. Everything that goes well for you, all of your achievements, successes and triumphs — no matter how small — recognise them and take note. So, you develop a practice whereby you anchor the positive experiences, thoughts and emotions you have about yourself and your life. And you can then use these anchors as reference points that you can call up in your mind to serve as affirmations of your strengths, abilities, competencies and the positivity you have in life.

For example, if you made an excellent public speech and wanted to make an anchor point from this, you can go through your memories and recall the setting and remember the various elements. In particular, remember how you felt and find a peak moment when you felt at your best. Is there any particular visual image, word, smell, taste or sound that you remember from that peak moment? Synthesise these elements into a snapshot from your memory that you associate with the peak feelings you had.

You can then pull up this snapshot in your awareness whenever you want to. So, you simply think of the snapshot and recall your feelings of strength. You use it as an anchor point that allows you to tap back into and reaffirm your peak feelings of confidence and elation. You can pull your past feelings into the present moment in order to assist you.

Change and Spontaneity

Over the past ten minutes — your body has made changes, your thoughts have been changing and your feelings have changed. These changes have most likely been subtle, but the point is, you are in a state of impermanence — you are always changing. If you identify aspects of yourself as rigid and unchanging, then you are overlooking your natural propensity to change and you are limiting yourself. Think for a few moments about how much you have already changed throughout your life. Change is natural.

Who you think you are is to a large extent simply your conception of who you are; based on your interpretations and beliefs. It's a construction, formed from memories. It is natural to have these conceptions, but if you believe them to be permanent then you restrict yourself.

Try not to have too many opinions about yourself. Try not to form too many mental assessments about yourself. Allow yourself to flow naturally as situations arise. Allow yourself room to change and room to adapt to whatever life brings.

One of the fastest ways to perceive new beliefs about yourself is to have new experiences. In particular, new experiences that challenge you and stretch your abilities. Try something new each week, learn something new each week. Never confine yourself to only doing things that you know you are good at — push outwards and expand your horizons. Be creative.

What often happens, is a person's intellect devises a plan for them in life. This occurs because the intellectual mind prefers certainty and wants to know the outcome. But if you have too much structure in life, you can miss opportunities. You can also become so obsessed with the destination, that you don't appreciate the journey and you miss all the little joys in life. When you are present in the moment, you can be more spontaneous and decisive in life. You can better trust your instincts.

If you feel like your life is overly structured, you can try this exercise. Take a day to simply be spontaneous and follow your instincts and your inner feelings. So, maybe you walk out of your home, go to a bus stop, and you get on the first bus that arrives. You get off at a stop you feel drawn by. You end up walking around, going into a shop, buying a frisbee, walking to a park, admiring the flowers, observing the ducks. And then you make friends with a stranger, play an enjoyable game of frisbee and go to a pub with them for lunch. What a great day! As people frequently say, the best experiences often aren't planned and couldn't have been planned.

CHAPTER THIRTEEN

Bridging the Gap to Authenticity

To be authentic, is to be who you really are, and when you can access the quintessence of who you really are — the version of yourself that is genuine and real — you will be amazed at how easy your life becomes.

But due to the way you were raised by your parents and society, it's likely the case, you've been steered away from your true and authentic self for much of your life. Perhaps you were passionate about certain subjects at school, but you were told they were not important and that you would struggle to make enough money, and so you neglected your passions and followed a different path. Maybe you excelled in a particular job and found yourself on a career path due to your abilities, but you feel unfulfilled, and you often wonder about and yearn for something different.

All too often, people end up doing what they think they ought to be doing in life, instead of doing what they really want to do. They make compromises based on what their family and friends think. They make decisions based on which career paths are most accepted, aggrandised and rewarded in society. People often head for status and financial security, and compromise on their inner values and beliefs. But this tends to leave them with a sense of being unfulfilled and out of control. Have you compromised too much? Are you living someone else's dream? Are you genuinely motivated by intrinsic reasons to do what you're doing in life?

If you are not making any headway towards honouring who you really are and doing what you really want to do, then an inner conflict can develop and begin to weigh you down. At some level, you will feel like something just isn't right, like you're not doing what you're supposed to be doing.

It is one of the great travesties of our times, as there are millions of people around the world doing things that they have no interest in and no passion for. This is creating all sorts of issues, as people are often filled with regrets and doubts about the compromises they have made. Compromises, that resulted in them pushing to the side their own inner motivations and passions to instead follow someone else's dream, someone else's version of what is acceptable and safe.

We live in a world where individuality is rarely encouraged, a world where people are homogenised through education curriculums and cultural norms and values. People are often afraid to step outside of the conventions they find themselves in, and this is especially true when there are added social pressures dictated by oppressive governments or religious orders. As time goes by, people can become so blinded by social conditioning, so compliant with the forces of conformity, that they almost completely forget what they were passionate about, about what they felt inspired by, and about what gave them a sense of purpose and meaning.

If you take away the influence of social pressure, who are you? If you take away the influences of your parents, your friends, your colleagues, your teachers, the media, the culture, the government. If all these influences were stripped away, what would be left?

Much of what you have learned from the influential people in your life is of course very useful. We naturally learn from imitation and we naturally assimilate beliefs, values and behaviours from other people, especially when we are growing up. Yet, we can become so clouded over by these influences that we can lose touch with our uniqueness and our individuality. And if this happens, we begin to act simply as robots, operating on a limited script that has been programmed for us by our major influencers.

The primary cause for this clouding is a perceived need for approval. So, in order to feel approved and accepted, we comply with social rules, standards and conventions. We yield to social pressure and end up conforming. Our pretences in life are usually rooted in our perceived need to please others by complying with the status quo of 'normal'. And people quickly learn how to fit in and how to act in certain ways that earn them social credits and status in groups.

Partly, this function of conformity originated from the safety of being part of a group — a tribe. In many ways, it is an evolutionary survival strategy. Being ostracised from a tribe was not in our ancestors' best interests due to threats from sabre tooth tigers and competing tribes. So, they tended to strive to be accepted in order to gain support and protection from others. But are these kind of threats relevant to you today? We have to question whether our motivations to be accepted and socially approved are driven by a false sense of insecurity. We have to recognise when we are compromising our individuality unnecessarily.

Without plunging too much into psychological jargon, your *ego* can be considered the part of you that wants to present itself to people in a particular way. It's the part of you that is self-conscious about how others perceive you. It's the part of you that reacts to your insecurities. And it is your ego that can lead you away from being authentic; in the pursuit of pleasing others and appearing a certain way to others. Yet, over time, a person can identify so much with their ego's presentation, that this presentation becomes their identity, and they lose touch with their authenticity.

When people ask, "What do you do?" How do you answer? Do you immediately tell them your job title and the name of the company you work for? Or do you tell them something about your personality and what you are passionate about? What a resume says, is usually not an honest representation of a person's authentic self. Yet, for many people, this is the identity they present to the world in order to fit in and gain other people's approval.

Being Genuine

You cannot become authentic if you are constantly having to change your appearance and behaviour simply for the sake of feeling accepted. You have to rectify this by being genuine. So, you think, talk and act in a way that is true to yourself, regardless of whether you'll be accepted by others or not.

Firstly, you've got to drop the pretence, you've got to be honest with yourself — you've got to take a good look at your inner psychology and go through a process of introspection.

And this doesn't mean being overly analytical or critical of yourself, but it means to look at yourself, without judgement, and peel back the layers to discover your true self.

Question yourself. Where do your beliefs, ideas and values come from? Can you trace back their roots? How much of you is original? How much of what you do in life is due to conformity? How much of what you do is solely to please others and fit in? Is the job you work at representative of anything to do with your personality? What is truly meaningful to you? What makes you genuinely happy?

You have to get in underneath the reasons for why you have certain attitudes, motivations and desires. Why do you want certain things? Why do you want to be like certain people? Why do you want to be perceived in certain ways? Are your desires genuine? Or are they projections of your ego's insecurities?

As you begin to really look at yourself in terms of why you think in certain ways, why you act in certain ways and why you say certain things; you will gradually start to perceive yourself from a more objective perspective. You can then start to see the difference between your true motivations and those that have been foisted upon you by your insecurities.

You can try this exercise. At the end of the day, run through in your mind the significant moments of the day and do this from a third person perspective, a bit like you are watching clips of a movie with yourself in. By taking time to bring your awareness outside of yourself, you will gain greater insight into your behaviours.

Look to identify how you were thinking, talking and acting — and assess each situation for whether you acted authentically or whether you were disingenuous or fake. In those situations where you felt you were not acting authentically, ask yourself, why? What was it about that situation that held you back? Then imagine yourself in that same situation acting as you genuinely would have liked to. How does that feel?

What you are looking to assess, is how you can be more genuine and authentic in your life. The key to authenticity, is to act of your own volition and not out of conformity or social pressure.

How many times have you come up with all sorts of excuses to justify why you *have* to do something? How many times have you tried to force yourself to feel a certain way? How many times have you spent an inordinate amount of time trying to find positives about situations that drain you and don't make you feel good?

All of this begins to pile up in your inner psychology. It is your ego trying to dominate, but all it can do is overlay more and more layers of justifications. The result is usually confusion. Confusion, because of the conflict between your genuine feelings and the incongruent overlays planted by your ego.

The ego is driven by its perceived need to resolve insecurities. So, it can push you around in the pursuit of money, status and prestige in order to satisfy its requirements. And if you allow it to dominate your mind, you can lose sight of what has genuine meaning to you.

It is healthy to have desires and ambitions, and the ego certainly has a function and can serve to motivate you. But the ego is never satisfied whilst it is still being alerted by a mentality of worries, discontent and doubts. So, if you are only motivated by your ego's yearnings to resolve your insecurities, you'll be chasing your tail forever. And this unrelenting dissatisfaction can lead to a sense of being out of control.

To go beyond the insecurity of the ego, you have to make an effort to appease it through reassurance. You have to resolve your inner conflicts.

So, you reassure yourself by recognising your strengths, skills, accomplishments and resources. By identifying what is going well in your life, and by being grateful for what you have, you can experience more contentment, and this will alleviate your insecurities.

You also have to assess whether any of your expectations, desires and opinions are causing you to feel insecure. Make an effort to neutralise any unease you feel about yourself or your circumstances. Focus your attention on the present moment, and don't allow yourself to languish in discontentment.

Take time to understand yourself and become assured by your own beliefs, interests and values. Root out any social conditioning and cultural programming that is not serving you, and align yourself with what has authentic meaning to you.

You also have to eliminate confusion and doubt. You have to train yourself to make wholehearted decisions and commitments. Otherwise, you can end up flickering in the limbo of discontentment due to confusion and doubt. Assure yourself with genuine reasons for why you are doing something, and then you can avoid unnecessary inner conflict.

For example, you may choose to take a job that you have little authentic interest in, but you recognise that you do authentically need to get paid! So, you can appease yourself and avoid inner conflict by assuring yourself about the reasons for your decision. You take the job, get paid, but, importantly, you do not give up looking for alternative ways to express your authenticity.

Never surrender to being an automaton where you feel out of control, being swept along helplessly. You have to break free of the simulation of conformity and take responsibility for your authenticity. So, regardless of what situation you find yourself in, make sure you are pushing in some way towards what you genuinely want in life.

When you are acting from your authenticity; your motivations and your actions will not require a whole load of justifications. There will be a harmony between your thoughts and your feelings, and because there is no friction between them, your ego will quieten. You'll transcend your inner conflicts and you'll feel coherent and composed.

For you to live authentically, you are going to have to be assertive and you are going to have to live a life that is self-determined. A life where you govern your own thoughts, words, feelings and actions. A life where you feel in control of the choices you make.

Being in control of your life means acting of your own volition. So, you do what you do in life because you decide what to do based on the meaning, value and purpose that you recognise. You make commitments in alignment with what is genuinely meaningful and valuable to you. You become true to yourself by honouring your word. You feel content to be yourself and you are strong enough to hold true to your own convictions.

It's not about being right or wrong, it's simply about being real and genuine. It's simply about recognising your own values, beliefs and observations — and being able to act on these without feeling any friction about doing so.

Authenticity is not about being self-righteous. And people don't necessarily need to know about your values, beliefs and observations — they don't necessarily need to know why you are acting in certain ways. To escape the prison of conformity, it is often best to slip out the side door quietly. Otherwise, certain people in your life may try and stop you from making a run for it!

Once on the path of authenticity, you do not crave approval or acceptance from others. You respect their views, but are not contorted by them if they conflict with your own. Other people's opinions are not required to validate you. So, you do not make decisions solely to please people. And you understand that the people who really care about you, will support you whether you listen to them or not. You become committed to learning and evolving in your own way, without comparing yourself to others.

If someone criticises you, you can respect their opinions, but you do not automatically adjust your behaviour in order to please them. You can take on board their criticism and assess it, but if it does not correlate with your inner values and beliefs, then you carry on in your own way. You openly admit when you make mistakes, but do not depreciate yourself. You develop a fortitude, whereby you can stand strong in your authenticity.

When you are authentic and genuine, you naturally become meticulously honest with people. And you let them know what you think and how you feel as necessary. You set boundaries with people when appropriate, and when required, you are assertive about your needs.

When you feel the need to express yourself, you are not stifled by worrying about offending people. You express your thoughts and feelings calmly and sincerely. You are not afraid of rejection or criticism. When you want something, you calmly explain precisely what you want and if necessary you explain the rationale for why you want it. You make requests, not demands.

For most of the time, you maintain your awareness in the

present moment, as that is where your authenticity is. Your past-self nor your future-self are the genuine authentic you that is present right now. So, you do not worry about decisions you have made in the past, or think too much about what could happen in the future.

Your authentic self is not set in stone. You are flexible and adaptable. You allow yourself to stretch the boundaries of who you are — to the far reaches of your potential.

When you focus attention on what is meaningful to you, you become attuned with your authentic self. When you take time to turn your concentration on yourself; you realise your own authentic values and needs. Then you break free from the constraints of the collective mindset. Then you can decide what you truly want in life and how you are going to do it. You bridge the gap between — who you think you should be and who you truly are. You bridge the gap between — what you think you should do and what you genuinely want to do.

Role Expectations

We all have to take on certain roles at times in our lives. Job roles are the primary example, and we usually end up having to contort ourselves to fit the expectations of the job description. But you should never lose sight of the distinction between your authentic self and the role you are playing. If you over-identify with roles you play in life, you can lose touch with your own individual needs. You can get stuck in a box.

People can also fall into certain role expectations that they don't necessarily have a job manual for. Yet, they end up conforming to socially expected standards. For example, the role of a father, a mother, a wife, a husband, a best friend — all of these roles come packaged with certain expectations. Even the role of being a child comes with certain expectations.

We have to exercise some caution when holding expectations of people. Role definitions, social standards, labels, diagnoses and stereotypes can all have profound effects on people. In the field of psychology, it has been found that if people are labelled as having dyslexia, depression, attention deficit disorder or any other psychological label, they will often end up conforming to the characteristics associated with these labels. That isn't to say these people don't fit certain quotas used to distinguish psychological conditions, but the act of labelling them, can limit their own expectations of themselves and restrict them from making changes.

If we are labelled, we can end up conforming to other people's expectations. And people often think they have to live up to other people's expectations in order to be approved and accepted by them. But we should try and break free of these expectations, especially if they are constricting.

The more we conform to labels, the harder it can be to break free of them, and we can end up internalising these labels as self-beliefs. Were you labelled and stereotyped at school? Are you labelled and stereotyped by your family? By your work colleagues? The quiet one, the weird one, the funny one, the clever one, the troublesome one?

As a child, you will have changed around the age of two to three years old. You became a toddler and broke free of the baby label. You rebelled and pushed against the expectations of your parents, who may well have been a bit surprised and were still treating you like a baby. Breaking free of labels and other people's expectations is natural.

If you are around people who label you, you can become regressive; you can slip back into conforming to their expectations — you can slide back into acting like your past self. This can lead to inner conflict if a friction is generated from the pressure to perform to the role. But a person may fear if they deviate from their expected role they could be rejected.

If you feel under any sort of duress to perform to a role, then you have to question why that is. Usually, it is due to insecurities about what might happen if you stepped out of the socially accepted parameters of the role. You have to rationally assess your need to conform to these roles and look for ways to instigate a balance, especially, if you are feeling overwhelmed, and want to break free.

For example, maybe you're a housewife, but you're fed up of doing the housework and want to break free of this role and do something else. But you may be under pressure from other people's expectations of your role, and so, you need to communicate your needs to these people.

What tends to happen, is people let the friction build up and then they get to a breaking point and suddenly change without communicating beforehand. So, they reach their limit, and decide they no longer want to live within the confines of their labels and roles. However, this can be a shock to people in their life who were not expecting them to change so abruptly.

It is best to be delicate and to communicate to the relevant people in your life. To calmly express your feelings and request what you want. Often, you will find that simply by authentically expressing your feelings and stating your needs, people will accommodate you. You can redefine your roles and still ensure that everyone is happy. You will then probably kick yourself, thinking, "Why on Earth didn't I say something earlier!" Don't be afraid of appearing weak if you simply need a break. And don't expect people to know what you need if you don't tell them.

You do have to compromise to a certain extent in life, especially with those you have commitments and responsibilities with. But you can still choose to negotiate your own path. And it helps to also respect other people for what they truly want in life. Allow people to change and be open to them changing. Don't label people and place rigid definitions on them. Help other people to change by holding a space of non-judgement open for them. Even if this makes you feel a little uncomfortable — allow people to break free from role expectations and to follow their authenticity.

CHAPTER FOURTEEN

Finding Meaning & Purpose

What do you really want in life? To truly answer this question, you have to explore your inner values, your interests and your passions.

What makes you feel happy? What makes you feel fulfilled? What gives you a sense of excitement and enthusiasm? What gives you a sense of prosperity? What really matters to you? What do you enjoy? What do you feel motivated to do? What inspires you and makes you feel passionate?

And why? Why do certain activities make you feel these positive emotions? What do they mean to you? Why do you derive meaning from these activities?

For example, is it the sense of autonomy that you feel? Or perhaps it is the sense of contribution or responsibility, learning, achievement, progress, challenge or connection?

Take some time to reflect on and answer the above

questions. If you write down the answers, this will enable you to further understand what is meaningful to you.

In the search for purpose, you are looking for ways you can express through action what is meaningful to you. The outcome of this meaningful expression is the purpose. In other words, identify what is meaningful to you and then decide what you will do with it — what purpose will you apply it to.

Research into purpose suggests to look for activities where there is an overlap of meaning, pleasure and strengths. So, a sense of purpose is found via action that:

- You feel is meaningful.
- You find enjoyable.
- Utilises your strengths.

People tend to gradually refine their sense of purpose by working towards goals and aspirations. In the pursuit of their aspirations they realise — their strengths and abilities, what makes them happy, and what gives them a sense of meaning. These understandings then provide a more defined and purposeful direction in life.

For example, a skilled musician may discover meaning and enjoyment from teaching people how to play instruments. And so, they make a transition. They perform less, and focus more of their time and effort on teaching music.

There will be numerous ways you can experience purpose in life. Sometimes an epiphany does happen — a profound realisation about the path you want to take in life. But more often, it is a journey of realisation after realisation whereby you engage with life. You try new ideas, new skills, new jobs, new activities that lead you to develop, grow and discover new forms of meaning and purpose.

Maybe you struggle to think of anything you do in life that is really meaningful. But perhaps what you are currently doing is a stepping stone towards an aspiration that does promise authentic meaning and purpose for you. Sometimes, you need to step back and look at the bigger picture and be patient. So, you derive meaning and purpose from the steps you are taking in life, that are leading you towards a more fulfilling experience of meaning and purpose.

But you do have to decipher what is truly meaningful to you.

For example, many people want to be rich and successful, yet many wealthy and highly successful people feel unfulfilled and unhappy. And many people with very little money or relative success feel fulfilled and happy. The reasons behind these distinctions are usually found in the levels of meaning and purpose people experience.

People will often strive to make progress to get to where they believe they need to get to. But often, when they finally arrive — they don't feel satisfied, and they realise that actually it wasn't really what they wanted after all. This is commonly referred to as a mid-life crisis, but it can occur at any age in adulthood. It is an epiphany that happens when a person realises they have been living a life that has little intrinsic meaning.

A person has to learn about themselves and contemplate what is genuinely meaningful to them. They can then transcend their social conditioning and the forces of conformity, and begin an authentic quest for meaning and purpose. When you align your actions in life with your deepest values, interests and passions; a sense of meaning and purpose will naturally arise. It is up to you to make choices that will lead you to experience this.

If you recognise that you feel no authentic meaning in

what you're doing in life, then you should take action to change. And remember, just because you are good at something doesn't necessarily mean you should do it. Just because you've been on a career path for many years and the thought of changing track is daunting, doesn't mean you can't change and be successful.

But it is also worth keeping in mind, that in order to experience meaning, you don't necessarily have to change what you are doing in life. Maybe you can just change your perspective. What we consider meaningful is contingent on our own sentiments and attitudes.

I met a man once who worked in the oil industry. He was wealthy and successful, but he said he wanted to leave his job. When we talked about what exactly he didn't like about the job, it transpired it was the industry itself. He'd seen the horrors of oil pollution and he believed that greener more sustainable energy sources were the way forward. He had developed an inner conflict, as working for big oil was no longer compatible with what was meaningful to him, and he therefore didn't feel like he was serving any positive purpose in his job. Although, he did appreciate the challenges his job presented and he especially enjoyed the friendships he had made with many colleagues. The salary was rather good too.

As we talked, I suggested that perhaps he could stay and make it his mission to change the industry from the inside. To do what he could to encourage the company to transition towards more ecologically minded business models. His face instantly lit up, he had never stopped to think about this. We discussed that he should put a time limit on his efforts and work towards some goals. If there was no progress after a certain time then he could revert to the plan of leaving. He was already coming up with ideas as we continued talking. I'm not sure how it all went for him, but the big oil companies have been gradually transitioning over the years since. What I did witness, was how this new sense of meaning and purpose reinvigorated this man and provided him new direction and motivation.

A friend of mine is head chef at a posh hotel in Ireland. He believes that sourcing food from local suppliers provides him with the best quality produce, but also supports the local businesses. This requires a lot more effort and coordination, as opposed to what many other chefs do, which is simply order everything from a centralised supplier. But supporting local businesses and getting fresh local produce provides my friend with a deeper sense of meaning and purpose.

People can become dissatisfied in life because they regard the things they do as meaningless. However, if they switch their perspective, it is often possible they can find meaning. It is often a matter of recognising that meaning can be derived from *how* you do things, rather than *what* you do.

Everything has some kind of meaning if you can see it. And if you act with purpose, you can appreciate the meaning in almost anything you do. Can you think of new ways to experience meaning and purpose by changing how you do, what you do? Or by simply changing your perspective about what you already do?

Many people tend to overlook the meaning and purpose in their life, but when they really think about it, they usually realise their life is rich in meaning and purpose. Take some time to reflect on all the things you do in life that have meaning and purpose.

Perhaps you are a cook at a school and yet it feels very mundane and meaningless. But look at the opportunity you have been given to feed all the children and to keep them nourished and healthy. Maybe you could derive some more meaning by making some changes to further help these kids.

Perhaps you are a manager in a bank and you feel demoralised by the monotony. Yet, can you derive some meaning by bending a few rules to provide a loan to the young business owner coming in later?

Certainly, there are different levels of meaning that we can perceive. And as you change in life, your perspectives will also change. What you feel is meaningful and enjoyable will change, as will your abilities and strengths. Perhaps this will result in you appreciating what you do in new ways or perhaps you will change direction in the pursuit of new forms of meaning and purpose.

We do have inherent needs to feel relatively secure, to feel a sense of autonomy, a sense of connection with others, a sense of progress and accomplishment — and you have to factor in these needs when pursuing meaning and purpose in life. You do have to understand yourself and your needs, and find a balance. For example, maybe you go ahead and pursue something that has meaning for you, but you end up feeling lonely or wind up with money issues. You have to be prepared to make adjustments to find balance and rectify your needs. Perhaps you can push ahead and accept some compromises or maybe you will need to make changes.

The people who feel happiest and most fulfilled have found ways to live in alignment with their own principles and values, whilst engaging with their interests and passions — and also getting their needs met. What you are ideally looking for, is a way to express your talents and skills, whilst experiencing authentic meaning and purpose.

But keep in mind that doing things in life you find meaningful, is not necessarily going to be easy and fun. Look through history at the hardship and resistance that many people endured whilst striving to make positive changes. But they persevered. They followed their passions and applied their skills because of the meaning they derived, and because they believed the purpose was important and worthwhile.

Some people are content with the meaning and purpose they derive from their hobbies or from their roles and relationships in life For example, the role of being a parent. What is clear, is that it is important for people to experience some authentic meaning and purpose in their life, and this can be achieved in many ways, and not solely through what job they do.

One of the most reputed ways to reach a deep sense of meaning and purpose is to pursue a path whereby you are making a positive difference in some way. Where you are serving others or where you are making a contribution to a wider cause that is bigger than your own.

Studies have revealed that a person can achieve a greater sense of meaning by improving the well-being of others. People feel most nourished when they recognise how their efforts are having a positive effect on others — when they feel they are adding value to the world.

Look to see how you could provide for your own individual needs, whilst also directing your energy outwards in service to other people or a wider cause.

CHAPTER FIFTEEN

Pursuing Aspirations

Setting goals in life can make you more focused, efficient and organised, and therefore more resilient to challenges that may arise. Goals help you to appreciate the present moment and enjoy the journey; as you know where you are going and therefore don't procrastinate by worrying about an uncertain future. They provide a roadmap and can give you a sense of development and progress as you move towards them and beyond them.

Goals that are aligned with your inner values, interests and passions are going to be easier to immerse yourself in and find flow with — as opposed to goals you may feel pressured to pursue. Focusing on goals that imbue a sense of growth, development, connection and contribution are much more likely to motivate you and enhance your well-being, than goals that are purely based on monetary gain and status.

Think more about what you want to do, rather than about

what you feel you have to do. And do your best to resist social pressures that can divert you from your authentic aspirations. Identify what it is you want to do and pursue it. By doing this, you will gain a sense of control over your life that will naturally increase your confidence.

If you pursue goals that are not in concordance with who you really are and what you really value in life, you will likely feel dissatisfied.

Question yourself about your goals and aspirations. Do you feel uncertain about them, unmotivated to proceed, pressured by others, restricted by thoughts solely about money?

Or do you feel a sense of excitement, deep interest and meaning? Do you feel your goals reflect who you are? Do your goals challenge you in rewarding ways? Do you feel empowered by pursuing your goals? Do you feel you are working with your talents and gifts?

A useful exercise, if you are not sure what to focus on, is to unload your mind of all your aspirations. So, you write down all of your ideas, interests, desires, strengths, resources, inspirations and ambitions. Even all the vague ideas that have floated around at the back of your mind. Include any unfinished projects you haven't fully let go of and also any plans that you regret not pursuing earlier in your life. Get it all out of your mind and onto paper.

Then, look to see if you can identify the ideas and aspirations that provide you with the greatest sense of meaning and purpose. Cast aside any doubts and fears you may have. Just see if you can recognise the items on your list that you feel an authentic connection with. And do remember to be attentive to your feelings and emotions. Check in with yourself about how an idea feels to you. Don't over intellectualise this exercise. Try not to frame your ideas too much in terms of rigid 'career paths' — think more in terms of what you feel passionate about.

In your own time (this can be a process over days or weeks) begin to place all your ideas into three columns. Title the three columns as No / Yes / Later.

The purpose here is to decide to either — let go of an idea, commit to it and take action, or agree to delay it. For those items that end up in your *Later* column, schedule in a time when you will do something in relation to it. This can be simply taking an hour to research the idea more. For those items in your *No* column, consciously affirm to yourself that you are letting these ideas and aspirations go. "I am now fully letting go my idea of becoming an astronaut." It will also help to discard any materials, documents and computer files that you'd collected in relation to this idea you are letting go of. The items in your *Yes* column are those that you are keen to take action towards straightaway.

This exercise allows you to explore all your ideas and aspirations, but then it also encourages you to make some decisions. There is nothing wrong with entertaining lots of ideas in your mind, but it can begin to weigh you down if no action is being taken. The process of letting go and scheduling releases you from this burden and allows you to feel organised and focused.

In order to truly focus on goals, you have to organise your mind and then commit your attention to what you decide you want to do. People are often quite vague with their aspirations or they change their mind too frequently. In both instances, they will struggle to focus and make progress. It is much better to crystallise your ideas as best you can, and then decide whether or not you will work towards them. If you decide to work towards them, decide when and schedule it. If you decide the idea is not something you want to pursue, ensure you let it go completely.

Once you have some clarity about the ideas and aspirations you want to pursue, you can start to plan the steps involved to get yourself there. It is important to separate your aspirations into small steps on the journey. As you proceed, you will begin to accumulate the achievements of each small step and will then gather momentum. This will increase your confidence and enthusiasm about moving closer towards your aspirations.

Be specific about your goals and break each goal down into small steps. Then engage yourself in the experience of accomplishing each step.

You have to believe the steps you are working on are achievable. But try not to drift off into concerning yourself about how you are going to achieve later steps that may at first seem unachievable. Every good plan there has ever been has come with elements of uncertainty. But if you keep moving forward, achieving what you can, then doors will open, opportunities will present themselves, and it is very likely you will be able to achieve those later steps or find a way around them.

Plan goals in stages whereby you have a list of goals that you make for each month, but then you also have a six month and possibly even a one-year overview plan as well. Schedule tasks for every day you can commit to your goals. Keep your plans up to date and keep a copy on your desk, coffee table, fridge, computer desktop or up on a wall — anywhere you will regularly notice it. And that also goes for anything related to your goals. For example, if you are learning an instrument and want to practice everyday, don't leave the instrument in a cupboard, leave it out on the table or somewhere where you'll keep noticing it. Bring what you are focusing on into the forefront of your life.

Be aware that making adjustments to your plan is inevitable and so be prepared to be flexible. Also, perhaps your aspirations will change. This often happens when people embark on a journey — they end up finding a different path to turn onto, and realise that it leads to a place more suited to them. Without committing to the initial path though, the new one would never have been found. Sometimes in life, it is best to simply proceed, even if you are not completely sure where you'll end up.

If you currently feel you have to work a job as a survival necessity or you feel stuck in some way — take initiative and instigate some movement towards aspirations that are aligned with your inner values and passions. Even if it is just for a few hours a week to start with. Take at least one action a day, no matter how small, and you will begin to develop momentum. You could research some ideas, join a relevant group or course, begin to plan and structure the steps to take, and also assess the benefits you will gain.

As you move towards your aspirations, it is often a good idea to change other aspects of your life to reinforce your momentum towards change. It might be worth reflecting on what has been stopping you from making changes in the past. Are there changes you could make in your life that would enhance your abilities to achieve your goals? Perhaps you could change your diet to be more health conscious, exercise more, meditate or you could contact people who could help you. In other words, if there are aspects of your life that you can change, and you think these changes will assist you in your journey towards your aspirations, then do it, make the changes.

Honour the changes you are making by getting rid of the clutter in your life — have a clear out of your belongings and radically organise. As much as possible, stop doing things you don't want to do and seeing people you don't want to see. Take control of your life by focusing on what is important to you and prioritising your time appropriately.

Come up with personal reasons for why completing your goals is essential for you. What is on the other side of you completing your goals that is irresistible? Why do you simply have to make your aspirations happen and bring them into reality? Imagine how your life will be different when you complete your goals. Imagine how you will feel, and allow these imaginations to encourage and motivate you.

Ideally, you want some level of excitement to be generated from the journey of pursuing your goals, but inevitably there will be some mundane tasks that you will have to accomplish along the way. If any mundaneness starts to impede on your motivation, remember your reasons for doing what you're doing. Step back and look at the bigger picture. Draw on the excitement generated by the thoughts of completing your goals and by moving closer to the future changes that excite you.

If you are not feeling challenged or if your goals are not stretching your capabilities, then you may not feel a significant sense of achievement, and this could hinder your sense of progress. Get out of your comfort zone at times and remember to interpret any perceived struggles as important challenges.

Pursue excellence not perfection. Go easy on yourself by being patient and composed. Recognise that anything you perceive as a failure, is a valuable lesson on the journey. Don't concern yourself about it and don't take it personally, you are human, none of us are perfect! Just focus on refining your strengths. Be brave and tenacious.

Remember to recognise all of your achievements on the

journey toward your goals, no matter how small. Don't fall into the common trap of getting frustrated because you're not *there* yet. Don't bother berating yourself if you feel you're behind schedule. Find a balance, where you don't overwork and burn out, and you don't procrastinate and lose focus.

Don't trouble yourself by worrying about the outcome. Persevere with a calm mind that is focused on the task and dedicated to doing your best. When you are dedicated to doing your best, you will often find that you can go beyond your expectations and do even better.

Working with others can greatly enhance your progress. Even if you are working on a solo mission, it is often beneficial to have at least one friend or family member you can check in with about your progress and get some feedback from — and hopefully some encouragement and support also!

Happiness

Happiness can entail many things — a sense of peace, progress, achievement, connection, responsibility, autonomy, security, freedom. If you are considering what to do in life, never forget to assess what makes you feel happy.

You can take some time to answer these questions: What makes you feel happy? When are you happiest? What are you doing when happiness lasts the longest?

Keep in mind your answers when you are considering your choices about which goals and aspirations to pursue. All too often, people overlook the simplicity of pursuing happiness.

If you are not sure where to head for in life, don't worry too much about it. Maybe you could take some time out and travel for a while or maybe you could go and volunteer on an organic farm and live there for a season.

Sometimes, it is best to take the pressure off, lessen your ambitions and simply experience life. People who do this often report profound realisations and inspirations. And they might realise that all their grand ambitions were not actually going to fulfill them. For example, some people realise that simply living from the land in a sustainable community is what makes them feel happy!

I provide a list below of some common characteristics of happy people:

• Able to embrace change.
• Generous and kind.
• Working with others on a project with a shared goal.
• Creative and innovative.
• Equitable leaders.
• Learning a new skill or developing an ability.
• Confident and able to take some risks.
• Accomplishing goals and tasks.
• Achieving to a high standard.
• Going beyond expectations.
• Not limited by fears.
• Solution focused.
• Does not dwell on negative experiences, worry or complain.
• Able to admit mistakes and strive to learn from them.
• Resilient and persevering.
• Self-sufficient and independent.
• Takes solitude and privacy when needed.
• Able to remain calm.
• Dedicated to self-growth, learning and fulfilling potential.
• Feels in control of their life by working diligently towards goals and aspirations.

- Excited by exploring new experiences and ideas. Eager to live a fulfilling life.
- Feeling challenged and stretched.
- Can perceive positive meaning and purpose in life.
- Happy for other people's accomplishments.
- Social and open to forming friendships.
- Assertive when necessary.
- Authentic and unabashed.
- Doesn't identify with career more than personality.
- Tolerant, patient and respectful of others.
- Able to see the bigger picture and other people's perspectives.
- Grateful and appreciative of what they have.
- Able to forgive.
- Takes care of oneself in a loving and nurturing way.
- Lives in the moment.

Look to see if there is anything on this list that you could aspire towards to increase your sense of happiness in life.

CHAPTER SIXTEEN

The Synergy of Attention & Intention

Our sensory inputs are stimulated constantly by sights, sounds, smells, tastes, touch, thoughts and feelings. If we were attentive to all the external and internal stimuli, we would not be able to function efficiently; we would be forever distracted and unable to focus with undivided attention on a particular task.

The ability to focus attention and concentrate, whilst also filtering out distractions, is an innate quality. For example, in a room full of people talking, a new born baby will turn its head towards its mother's voice. We have an inherent ability to focus attention.

The brain is very adept at ordering and structuring information — it is constantly assessing and categorising incoming stimuli and will automatically vary our level of attention based on its calculations. This is mostly a function that evolved for survival purposes. And it is the reason why we find it easier to focus attention on things that have intrinsic value to us. When we perceive that something is important, we can sustain our attention more intensely and for longer periods. When we perceive meaning and purpose, we can focus our attention with more force.

Our ability to focus our attention can reveal what we are truly motivated by. You can probably think of examples of when you could concentrate very well because you were genuinely interested in a task or you were aware of the importance of being attentive. And you can also probably remember times when you found it difficult to sustain your attention because you did not deem the task to be interesting or important.

To maximise the force of attention, you have to recognise reasons for focusing your attention, and harness these reasons as your motivation. In particular, you can amplify this motivation by recognising how focusing your attention will serve your needs and the needs of others. Think about the meaning, purpose and value for what you are doing. And use this information to invigorate your motivation.

When you are genuinely motivated and can readily focus attention, you can enter into a state of flow. Flow, is when your attention levels peak and you enter *the zone*. During this state of flow, distractions are filtered out and a total immersion in what you are doing occurs. You can effortlessly sustain your attention. You feel at one with what you are doing — completely in control with no fear of failure. You can become so engaged that your perception of time changes.

If what you are focusing attention on is too easy or too challenging then distraction or apprehension can prevent flow. To enter into a flow state, it is best to focus on a specific goal that you feel is challenging yet also achievable. It is therefore a good idea to separate your goals into achievable steps, so that you can gain a sense of accomplishment and enter the flow state in each step.

The word attention comes from the Latin word, *attendere*, which means 'to stretch towards'. When you focus attention in a dedicated way, you reach out towards your focus and create a feedback loop, enabling higher levels of cognition and perception. Therefore, even when you are not consciously focusing your attention on the task, information is still being processed, assimilated and organised — allowing for greater insight and understanding. In a way, you become what you focus upon, you absorb it and permeate into it. Once this state of attention has been reached, information will appear in your dreams and will spontaneously arrive in your mind as eureka moments.

However, if your mind is dominated by worries, ruminations, opinions and judgements, you will find it difficult to access these heightened states of attention. And you will also miss much of what is happening in the real world.

If we aren't present in the moment when focusing on a task or communicating with people, this will undermine the quality of our performance and our relationships. There is little understanding or connection without diligent attention. By maintaining a mind uncluttered by thoughts and emotions, you can attain a much clearer awareness, from which attention can be focused more readily.

You have to develop a mode of attention where your conscious will has command and can readily filter out distractions and keep you focused. There are so many ways in which we can divide our attention unnecessarily. And especially nowadays, in our digital age, millions of potentially meaningless distractions are only a button click away. You have to limit distractions when you want to focus your attention. So, for example, put your phone on silent, turn off the TV and radio. The less irrelevant information your mind has to process, the better you will be able to concentrate on what is important to you.

Companies, government, friends, family members — many people will want your attention. But you have to set boundaries, and sometimes it is best to ensure you get time alone or solely with the people you are working with. We need to focus at times in our life, otherwise we can remain in a kaleidoscope of fleeting stimuli that prevents us from focusing our attention and making progress.

Here are some further tips for enhancing attention:

• Notice when your mind strays and then pull it back to the centre of your focus, keep doing this and you will ingrain the habit.

• If thoughts come to mind about another subject that you feel is important, take a quick note, and then refocus your attention.

• Start a task and just keep going even if you're not in the mood. Do a draft, even if you think you'll do it badly, just do it. A momentum will be initiated through perseverance and heightened levels of attention will kick in.

• Declutter and organise your living and working areas — create harmony. Ensure you have around you the things that are most relevant to your main focus.

• Take a short break approximately every 90 minutes. Ideally, find a quiet place, close your eyes and relax. This will allow your mental processes to assimilate and organise information; providing you with greater understanding when you return to consciously focusing your attention.

• During times of relaxation you can practice visualisation. You can bring your mental attention to working through the steps towards your objectives. So, you visualise yourself focusing on what you have to do. This will assist you to concentrate when it comes to actually doing it. And you may also have fresh ideas during the visualisation that can assist you.

- If you realise you are hindering yourself by focusing on negative thoughts and emotions, try to switch your perspective to more neutral or positive interpretations. Work with the advice I mentioned in earlier chapters about reducing worrying and processing emotions.

- Ensure you are well hydrated and that your diet is not too high in sugar or caffeine. Exercise a little each day as a base minimum.

- Tweak your memory and attention span through neuroplasticity games and apps. The app named Elevate is recommended.

- To increase your ability to concentrate, you can practice staring at one object without thinking about anything else. Just focus your attention on the object. See how long you can do it without losing focus. Practice until you can do it for at least two minutes.

- Make a schedule and set time-limits and deadlines. Having other people involved can create positive pressure and responsibility.

- Create an overview of small steps and structure your objectives. This will help you to maximise your attention by dedicating your focus on one task at a time.

Coherence and Intention

An intention is a premeditated choice to manifest a particular outcome. When applied with conviction, an intention becomes more than simply an aim or a desire, it becomes a power that can open the doors of possibility to unbounded potential.

To master intention, you have to become finely attuned to how your thoughts, words, feelings and actions are influencing your life. You have to understand that what you express through your inner sentiments and actions is then reflected in what events and circumstances unfold in your life. In a sense, we are making intentions all of the time, but often they are incoherent and fleeting. And then we wonder why we're not making any progress and why situations continue to arise that we don't really want.

To work with intention, you have to create a coherence between you and your intention. So, you have to align your thoughts, words, feelings and actions with the intention, and train yourself to shift any discord. You have to maintain the majority of your thoughts, words, feelings and actions as being conducive to fulfilling your intention.

If your thoughts are too scattered and dominated by worries; if the words you speak reflect doubt and disbelief; if your feelings are confused and anxious; or if none of your actions are converging towards the intention — you will impede your progress.

You have to compose and organise your thoughts and words into precise forms. You have to manage and centre your feelings so they are a coherent and positive influence. And you have to take action that is aligned and congruent with your intention. Essentially, you have to keep closing the gaps between you and your intention.

But you can't just force yourself to think positive thoughts or talk in a positive way and expect your inner feelings to change automatically. And it is your inner feelings that are most influential when it comes to working towards an intention. So, you have to gradually bring your feelings into alignment with your thoughts, speech and actions.

The easiest way to achieve this congruence is to work with intentions that have authentic meaning and purpose to you. When you really feel your intention is aligned with genuine purpose, you will feel good about it. When you feel good about it, you will naturally be able to align yourself with your intention.

The greatest sense of purpose comes from being in service to others. Thus, intentions with an altruistic purpose will be easier to align to. Take time to focus compassionately on others and yourself when making your intentions. Reflect on how your intended outcome will be beneficial for other people, as well as yourself.

A truly unyielding intention with unshakable purpose is a catalyst of creation. And once you have connected clear and precise thoughts to your intention, and aligned your feelings with deep meaning and purpose underlying your intention — all that remains is for you to act.

Intention is a tool to bring forth potential — it is the pull, as attention is the push — it is a reference point from which providence can open the doors of potential. Without using the force of attention, the potential of intention is limited. You have to take action and push toward your intention with a determined attention on the necessary action.

When you align to your intention and work the force of attention, miracles will happen. The right people will come into your life, opportunities will unfold, spontaneous healings will take place, synchronicities will guide you, a sense of higher purpose will fulfill you, a momentum will flow, doors will open and seemingly insurmountable obstacles will be overcome.

Your greatest challenge will be changing the patterns of your subconscious. You have to maintain discipline and no matter what comes up in your mind or in your life, you tenaciously continue to pursue your goals. And you continue to consolidate consistency in your thoughts, speech, feelings and actions in alignment with your intention. Then, bit by bit, your subconscious patterns will change to align with your intention. When this happens, there will be no more self-generated resistance and you will enter a flow.

Do not compose your intentions based on thoughts about what you lack. If you focus on what you don't have, then you align yourself to insufficiency. Instead, focus on being thankful and grateful for all that you have had, have and *will have*. When you are grateful, you become humble, and when you are humble, you won't be afflicted by the contrition of worrying, yearning or longing. You also won't fear losing what you have and will be content to take risks in the pursuit of your goals.

Importantly, when working with intention, you should let go of any attachment you may have about the end result. And you should let go of any yearning emotions about a time scale. So, it's like you make a wish without longing for it to come true — you hold a desire without worrying about the outcome of your desire happening.

You develop a silent trust. A trust, whereby you surrender into a deep reverence, and accept that what is meant to be will be. A trust, whereby even if your intentions aren't manifested exactly when or as you wanted, you accept with grace what you receive. And then, with humility, you can proceed with a new intention if you wish to.

Here are the steps for working with intention:
- Get specific on what you want. Do some research, reflect on it, write down ideas, draw them, collect relevant pieces

of information. Be aware of the potentials, don't limit yourself. Then refine your intention into a specific and succinct thought form that has authentic meaning and purpose to you. Be prepared to change your thought form as you hone in on what it is you genuinely want. Keep it simple yet specific. Condense it into a succinct sentence or even a single word that summarises your intention.

- Recognise how you will feel when your intention is manifested. What feelings are invoked by what it means to you? Imagine the outcome of your intention has already arrived. How do you feel? What are you grateful for? Explore these feelings in the present moment.

- Visualise the outcome of your intention and the reality you want. Visualise yourself and anything relevant to your intended outcome. Only imagine the outcome you want, not the process of getting there.

- In a meditation or when you are relaxed, focus on what you have discerned from the above three steps. So, you focus on your intention thought form, you invoke the feelings of your fulfilled intention and you visualise the outcome of your intention. Take at least ten minutes a day to focus on your thought form, whilst pulling in the feelings and visualising the outcome.

- Continue to consolidate consistency in your thoughts, speech, feelings and actions in day to day life. Align yourself with your intention and counter any discord. Before your daily intention meditation, review how things have been going. Commit to making any changes as necessary to close the gap and keep building the bridge to your intention. Let go of yearnings and worries. Trust. Compose yourself, and focus your attention on taking action and pursuing your goals.

When intentions are focused on communally they become more powerful. A group with a unified purpose can enhance the potential of any intention. Research shows that a group of between six and twelve people functions most optimally for amplifying intentions. The book titled *The Power Of Eight* by Lynne McTaggart explains much more about this topic, and you may be surprised to realise how much scientific literature there is about the power of intention. It is a very interesting read.

CHAPTER SEVENTEEN

Shadow Processes

The term 'shadow' was coined by the psychologist Carl Jung. According to Jung, the shadow constitutes elements within the mind that creep out and influence people in destructive ways. He proposed, that if people identify and discover these influences, they can correct them.

To identify and discover shadow traits, you start by looking at ways in which you react. Ways in which you react to yourself, circumstances and other people. What you are primarily looking for, are the reactions rooted in some kind of attrition with your desires.

For the most part, shadow reactions occur due to some form of insecurity. And what tends to happen, is people react to things that at some level they perceive as threatening, offensive or undesirable. It is usually the whim of the ego projecting it's discontent due to some kind of contradiction with it's expectations.

Fear of Loss

People often focus too much on their fears about loss. For example, they may fear a loss of security, attention, control or meaning. These fears can lead them to worry a lot, and these worries can lead them to act in unreasonable ways to prevent loss or compensate for their fears.

People who fear a loss of security can often become obsessed with saving money and will exploit every opportunity possible to get a free ride. Because of this, they can become greedy and mean. They'll cling onto their possessions to the point where their possessions end up owning them. They'll often cut corners and rip people off to save money. They will evaluate people only in terms of what value they present, and they will then exploit them and take advantage of them. They become selfish.

If a person feels threatened by other people, they may resort to sabotage and manipulation in order to protect their interests. For example, if a person is worried about losing their job, they may spread malicious and baseless rumours about some of their co-workers in an attempt to offset their own demise, by throwing other people under the bus.

The more you worry about loss, the more it weighs you down. And then you can't fully appreciate what you have as you're always worrying about losing it. You have to give up your yearning to control everything and learn to accept some uncertainty in life. When a person can accept the potential of loss, they can relax, and they won't have to succumb to dishonourable methods to protect their interests.

People who are very controlling will always want to get their way. They thrive from having control over others and imposing their will on others. And they will often react aggressively to any person or situation that threatens them.

They fear losing control.

In order to feel secure in their control, they will be obsessive in their attempts to maintain order and certainty. They will often create lots of rules. Then they'll also change these rules regularly to serve their whims. They'll be very demanding and will have inordinate expectations of people. Even when they are attempting to play nice, their passive aggression will be felt. They will often purposefully be disrespectful and vengeful by engaging in sarcasm, insults and punishments. They tend to take pleasure in finding ways to make others suffer in order to keep them subservient. They will attempt to dominate people's thoughts and beliefs by instilling fear about the consequences of not towing the line. They may also resort to bribery to ensure their control is not jeopardised.

The curious thing, is that people who are very controlling will often never be able to feel fully in control because other people will be constantly trying to usurp their control. People don't like being unduly controlled, and so in order to exert their own form of power, they will rebel. For example, a business with a dominating controller as the boss will usually be filled with staff who don't do what is expected, so, they'll turn up late, feign incompetence, and sabotage projects. And many of these behaviours are only occurring as a reaction to the dominance of the boss — it is the staff's way of trying to counter-balance and exert their own sense of control, and disempower the boss.

If you are in command of other people — you can choose to be an equitable leader and not be a domineering controller. Certainly, sometimes you will need to let people go and you will need to be assertive. But you can be in charge and still be respected by people without having to create conditions of fear, anxiety and reprisal.

Resentment

When a person is resentful, they will usually want something. And if they succumb to their shadow impulses, they may resort to rather unsavoury methods to get what they want.

For example, if someone is resentful of your wealth, they may over-charge you or rip you off in some way — they want to make you poorer and them richer. If someone is resentful of your status, they may try and take away your influence through sabotage, slander and gossip — they want to disempower you and empower themselves. If someone is resentful of your beauty, they may be cruel to you in the hope that you'll feel miserable and your beauty becomes diluted by negative emotions — they want to make you uglier so they can feel more attractive in comparison. If someone is resentful of your calmness, they may try and make your life stressful — they want you to feel stressed like they do and then they won't have to be resentful of your calmness.

Even if no interaction occurs, resentment can still create an inner friction for people who are judgemental. For example, a young backpacker travelling around on a shoestring budget may resent business men and women they observe, as they desire their status, achievement and wealth. But the business people may look at this backpacker and resent the freedom and spontaneity they have.

People will seldom admit this, but often what we resent people for, is actually what we want. It can therefore be very useful to identify what we find ourselves resenting other people for. Often, this will reveal what we want for ourselves. So, for example, a person may want more wealth, power, beauty, calmness or autonomy.

In order to ditch resentment, you accept your circumstances and neutralise any discontent, jealousy, bitterness or angst you have about other people. You then take action to get what you genuinely want — without infringing on other people.

Resentment can also lead to a sense of malaise whereby a person feels an ongoing rift of frustration, angst and unease. This is usually formed due to a deep seated sense of injustice or unfairness. For example, a person may feel resentment towards certain politicians and blame them for aspects of their life. They may feel resentment towards their colleagues because they think they work harder and deserve more reward. They may feel resentment towards the societal system in general and will therefore resent people who are actively participating in the system.

The inner angst of resentment can gnaw away at you, it's a drain of your energy. It's natural to sometimes get upset about the way things are, but if you allow these emotions to dominate, you can become bitter and resentful.

Instead of languishing in negative emotions, you can recognise the friction within you and channel that energy into taking positive action. But do not fall back into resentment if you recognise things are out of your control and you cannot change them.

When it comes to the political system, remember this time-honoured piece of English wisdom:

"Don't let the bastards get you down."

Importance

The modern world is obsessed with consumerism. People are conditioned to want stuff. This stuff is associated with status, and this status provides people with a sense of importance. But people can only feel important if they can compare themselves to others and feel superior. And people often seek ways to distinguish and separate themselves from others, in order to reinforce their sense of importance.

So, if they notice a neighbour has bought a new car, they can perceive this as a threat to their status, and so they go and buy a slightly more expensive new car. If their friend receives a diamond ring, they may desire an equally expensive or more expensive ring. If their colleague gets plastic surgery, they may desire an equally or even more substantial plastic surgery. On and on it goes. And due to the incessant celebrity culture that pervades the media, combined with increasingly insidious marketing techniques, there really is never an end in sight of people to compare with.

Someone always has something better than what you have, and this can make you feel insecure, if you allow it to bother you. The trick is to be happy for what other people have and also to be happy for what you have. If you end up thinking, 'I want what they've got' then you should question the roots of your desire. Is your desire simply about status and importance — because you want to feel equal or superior to the other person? Or do you actually have a genuine need for what the other person has?

Another aspect of importance, is how people perceive each other's status in society. This is usually wrapped up in the perception of what job they do and how much money they earn. People will often seek job positions solely for the power and prestige they provide. If they believe that the only way for them to feel secure, is to be in a position of power where they have control over other people, and are earning more money than other people, then that is what they will be propelled to do.

There is nothing inherently wrong with seeking power, prestige and money. But if you are pursuing these goals solely because you crave the sense of superiority and importance over others, then you are acting from the insecurities of your ego.

If your pride becomes wrapped up with a need to be perceived as important, then you are more likely to resort to shadow impulses to get what you want. Your sense of importance can lead you to become arrogant, selfish, disdainful and overly controlling. You can become reactive if you sense any threat to your status, and the thing is, you will never be satisfied so long as you crave importance. And there will always be someone who will irk your pride. And there will always be something that you can't attain or control.

I was in a car once and the driver was trying to come out of a car parking space, yet there was a stream of traffic and no one was letting him out. He began to become very impatient. He was banging the steering wheel with his fists and shouting at people. Eventually, someone gave way and let him pull out of the space and join the traffic queue. Yet, he was still fuming with indignation because his sense of importance had been scuppered by all the drivers who had not given way for him. Huffing and puffing, he noticed someone else pulling out of a parking space in the same situation as he had just been in. But instead of sympathising with this driver, he accelerated to close the gap and disallowed this driver to pull out!

This is the hypocrisy of importance. So, this man didn't stop to empathise with the other driver even though he had just been through the same experience and found it very frustrating. He was in a rush, but he didn't care in any way that the other driver may also have been in a rush. He deemed himself to be more important without a second thought about it.

Watch out for importance as it can lead you down the path of disdain and arrogance. And there will always be someone or some situation that will cause consternation and discontentment if you hold these attitudes and sentiments. And usually you'll meet them everyday, in every car park, in every venue of life. But if you don't care about being perceived as important, and you don't have a superiority complex whereby you've ordained yourself as being more deserving than others — then life becomes much easier!

It is best to be silent about your accolades and to not compare yourself to others. There is no need to show off. And there is no need to run around demanding people yield to you and acknowledge you're important. There is no need to prove you are 'better off' than the next person. There is no need to attain status solely for a sense of superiority you may get from lauding over others.

You can go beyond importance by being humble and cultivating within yourself attitudes of respect, tolerance and equitability. Remember, it's all relative anyway. For example, if a natural disaster occurs, all those who identified themselves as very important people are suddenly in the same situation as everyone else — swimming around looking for a tin of baked beans in the aftermath. Importance is only ever a temporary illusion granted by onlookers.

Prejudice

Prejudice is the harbouring of sentiments about other people due to preconceived opinions that are not based on reason or actual experience. It is the pre-judgement of people based on unsubstantiated evidence.

What tends to happen as a result of prejudice, is people hold generalisations and stereotypes about certain people and social groups. Race, ethnicity, nationality, gender, intelligence, status, class and wealth are some of the prime examples people often have prejudices about.

People may also discriminate against others based on their prejudices. This is usually because some kind of resentment or disdain has formed in their mind that can cause them to feel justified in behaving in certain ways. Sometimes, people don't even consciously act upon their prejudices, but they are so ingrained, that discriminatory behaviours occur spontaneously.

For example, a person may be very rude and condescending to a waiter in a restaurant, simply because they deem them to be inferior. But then the waiter may have their own prejudices, and is also impolite, due to being resentful of the status and wealth they perceive the customer has, on top of, reacting to the customer's attitude. This is a typical example of the dynamics of prejudice. And the discrimination occurs due to pre-existing prejudices that are enacted upon due to disdain and resentment. The cycle then continues, as both characters think they have confirmed their preconceived opinions — yet usually they don't see how their own behaviour has influenced the other person's behaviour. And round and round it goes.

You have to recognise any prejudices you have and question the reasoning behind them. Do you have any evidence to support generalisations you make about certain people? Do you have any realistic justifications for treating a person in a certain way simply due to their appearance?

All too often, people make generalisations and judgements based on vague opinions and hearsay that they have no evidence to back up. But even if you do have evidence from past experiences, you do still have to be aware that your generalisations may be entirely wrong in the next instance. And therefore, you should be mindful, and make an effort to not act in discriminatory ways simply because of preconceived opinions you may have. And also, even if someone does act in a discriminatory way towards you, it doesn't mean you have to resort to discriminating against them. You have to transcend any impulses towards retaliation and vengeance if you want to attain inner peace.

When you stop identifying surface level differences and distinctions people have, then you can stop making judgements about them based on their appearance. And when you can accept that any prejudices or stereotype generalisations you have, may be completely inapplicable and inaccurate, then you can remain neutral, and treat people with impartiality.

If you see a man sleeping on a park bench, what assumptions might you make? But how do you know what this man has been through? How do you know this man has not recently pulled himself out of the most awful situation and lifestyle? He may have been through horrors you could not even imagine and may have accomplished things you would shiver at the thought of. You have to watch for judgement, disdain and indignation. Much of the time, you simply do not know what people have been through in life.

There was a social experiment done some years ago. A person working for the experiment, dressed up in clothes typical for a homeless person, walked through a busy town centre, pretended to have a heart attack and collapsed to the ground. Despite his continued groans, dozens of people walked past this man, some of them even stepped over him, and it wasn't for about ten minutes that someone knelt down to see if the man was alright. Then the researchers performed a twist on the experiment. They dressed the man up in an expensive suit to resemble a smart professional businessman, and he proceeded with the same routine. But, this time, when the man collapsed, several people came to his aid within seconds. Prejudices can lead people to be very cruel and discriminatory.

Through the aggrandisement of certain status symbols, people have become conditioned to judge people in certain ways. So, you have to unlearn this programming if you are to avoid making judgements based on people's appearances and impressions. You should also question the hierarchies of status in society. Just because someone has a certain qualification, license, credit rating, designer clothes and new car does not necessarily mean they have certain qualities that you may associate with these types of distinctions. And just because someone has zero qualifications, little money, old clothes and a tattoo does not necessarily mean they have certain qualities that you may associate with these types of distinctions.

What tends to happen, is people gravitate towards a particular social group that they identify with. And they can then perceive people outside of their group in derogatory ways. This elitism is very common and it can become very toxic if one group decides they need to impose their will on another. Indeed, this has been the excuse for many wars of aggression throughout human history. One group decides they are superior and should exercise their superiority by changing the other group. 'Regime change' as it is often referred to today in politically correct language.

So, you also have to watch out for any righteous opinions you may have about what is best for people. I'm sure you have no plans to raise an army or start a cult, but take a look to see if you have any strong desires to control what people should or should not be doing. And if you do, then question your logic, where have your opinions come from? Do you really know what is best for people?

You may think your opinions are correct, and maybe they are, but people often make assumptions that are based upon superficial understandings and prejudices. For example, they might assume that other people will want the same things that they want. Or they may think that other people need to be controlled in certain ways for the 'greater good'.

Take the example of those who demand people in developing countries are given western medicines and the children are sent to western style schools. Yet, such charitable programs often do not go as planned, as the recipients reject the assistance because they were actually content with their lives before the intervention. If someone is not asking for assistance, it is usually best to leave them be. You can come up with ideas and share them, but watch out for any yearning desires to control people's lives.

Another tricky aspect of prejudice, is the judgements we make about what people deserve. This can become very toxic also. If you hold sentiments about what people deserve, then you can enter into the framework of reward or punishment. This framework dictates that people have to prove their worth in order to get rewarded, or else they will be punished. In the legal system there are juries who weigh up the evidence in order to make judgements. But in terms of day to day life, people are often involved with the same type of judgement process. There is nothing inherently wrong with this, but the point is, that you have to be mindful of your prejudices and the validity of your evaluations.

Let's say you are in a restaurant and the waitress gets your order wrong, so when you leave, you judge that she doesn't deserve a tip. But how do you know what this waitress has been through recently in her life? Maybe she has had a really hard time over the past week and had a simple lapse of concentration, which you have then, in a way, decided to punish her for.

You will often not have all the relevant information to accurately weigh up decisions about people. In circumstances where you don't have much information, it is best to simply treat people with dignity and respect.

Projections

If you find yourself reacting with anger, resentment or indignation because someone has offended you — look to see if you can identify any similar attributes in yourself. It is often the case that the attributes we don't like in others are the attributes we don't like about ourselves. And this is what actually fuels the emotional reaction. So, you can often learn about your own shadow traits, by monitoring your reactions to certain traits in other people. Think about what triggers you emotionally about other people. Have you resolved these traits in yourself?

If you are afraid of certain traits in others or you find them undesirable, then you will also, at some level, feel the same way about yourself if you have similar traits. The contemptuous reactions people can have about others are often a subversive way of compensating for the shame they have about their own traits. I've watched people become enraged about someone's dishonesty and five minutes later they are being dishonest, but they don't see the connection, they don't notice their own hypocrisy.

Another curious aspect of shadow work, is that people project their own traits onto other people. So, what people see in themselves, they suspect is also in others. For example, if someone short changes you, they may be thinking, "Well, they would have done it to me." Or if the roles were reversed, this person may be suspicious of being short changed, because they would short change you if they had the opportunity. So, you have to look at what you are projecting onto other people. Are you judging people based on your own characteristics and attitudes? If so, then this is another way for you to recognise your own shadow traits.

Also, you have to watch out for suspecting people of doing things, simply because other people in the past in a similar situation have done certain things. For example, you can't judge every plumber as being untrustworthy just because two plumbers in a row let you down and ripped you off.

And then, let's say, you're an electrician and get called out to a plumber's house — you shouldn't not provide them with courtesy and good service just because some other plumbers didn't provide you with courtesy and good service. And even if you end up at the house of one of the plumbers who ripped you off — you should still honour your agreement and provide a good service. And then, over a cup of tea, you can remind the plumber who you are, and ask them why your shower never got repaired! Because you've done a good job for them, this plumber will likely apologise and come straight round to your house and sort your shower out.

There are so many people who act in a tick for tack manner whereby they allow their own principles to become eroded by the dishonourable behaviour of others. They end up mirroring the dishonour and passing it on, despite being upset that it happened to them. So, you have to watch out for being vengeful due to past experiences. Some people are bound to be dishonourable and rip you off or let you down. But don't let that affect your own scruples. Rise above it, hold true to your principles and remain honourable. By living in this way, you'll often gravitate towards the people who will honour you in return.

What people judge each other for, they will often become. So, for example, a person may become angry because they react to someone else's anger. Or they may become callous as a result of someone being callous to them. The unfortunate thing, is that often these reactions are then passed on to others and then they pass them on to others. So, one guy sticks his finger up at someone driving in a traffic jam and an emotional reaction occurs. This incensed driver then arrives at work fuming, shouts at the manager, who then in turn goes and shouts at the staff, who then in turn shout at each other, and they all go home in a bad mood and shout at their kids! Be mindful to nip negative emotional reactions in the bud and not pass the buck.

Of course, there are times when emotional reactions are natural and authentic, and sometimes it is appropriate to react, and perhaps other people need to know how you feel and can learn from what you have to say. So, it's not about being passive all the time, it's about being authentic in the reasons for your reactions. It's about being mindful of whether you are reacting due to sincere and reasonable sentiments or whether you are reacting due to projections or shadow traits.

Practice spreading genuine goodness and kindness. When you are kind and respectful to someone, in most cases, you will inspire this person, and they will then be kind and respectful to the next person they interact with.

Communication Skills

Errors in communication are common, especially if tensions are high. To reach genuine resolution you have to reach a mutual understanding. In order to reach mutual understanding, you have to attain clarity.

During conversations about any disappointment or disagreement causing tension, it is good practice to paraphrase what you have understood the person to have said. You do this by listening to them and then calmly restating what you've understood them to have said. This then allows the other person to realise how they are being understood, and gives them the opportunity to correct any misunderstanding or inaccuracies. So, you listen and then, for example, say, 'If I understand you correctly, you are upset because...' and then you relay to them your understanding of what they are upset about.

You have to maintain an openness to seeing the other person's point of view, and by doing this you can better understand them and can develop an awareness of their needs. As you communicate in this way, you enter into an empathic rapport. By stepping into another person's shoes — you imagine the situation from their perspective — you listen to their words and see the world from their viewpoint — you attempt to feel what they feel.

To listen with empathy:
- Maintain soft eye contact.
- Hold a non-aggressive and open body language.
- Give your undivided attention, so turn off televisions or

devices as appropriate.

• Stay calm.

• Be genuinely interested in what they have to say and acknowledge them respectfully as they speak so they know you are listening.

• Think about how you can relate to what they have experienced.

• Stay compassionate and allow time for them to express their perspective and their feelings.

Reconciliation

One of the ways shadow traits are perpetuated is through the continuation of grudges and grievances. When a person holds grudges and grievances about other people, the emotions can weigh them down. And people often carry around their grievances like a ball and chain, and if a similar incident occurs, the weight of the ball then gets heavier as more grievances stack up.

If you are holding any grudges or grievances, then in order to regain inner peace, you have to clear the decks. You have to do what you can to mend your past grievances. Reconciliation occurs when you make peace with people. So, you make an effort to accept and forgive people that you have grievances with.

Of course, some actions are unforgivable, but for your own peace of mind, you should at least focus on accepting what happened so that you can move on. So, you surrender to the fact that whatever happened, happened in the past and cannot be changed. And you surrender to the knowing, that holding onto any grievances is futile and a burden to you. This way, you can start to release yourself of any anger, resentment or bitterness, and you can head towards a point of neutrality.

During this process, it may help to express certain things to people. The act of expressing how you have felt can help to release you from grievances. But don't expect anything in return. Don't hinge your acceptance on whether or not you receive an apology. If you are no longer in touch with these people, you could write a letter to them expressing how you have felt, and then bury it, burn it, or watch it float away with the current on a river.

You can also try this exercise when you are relaxed or meditating. Bring the person to your mind and imagine you are talking to this person. Express yourself — tell them how you have felt and what upset you. After you have explained yourself to this person and expressed any relevant emotions, look them in the eyes and tell them you accept what happened and that you are now letting it go. So, you might say in your mind softly, "I accept what happened and I forgive you. I am letting it go now." Then you say goodbye and in your imagination, you watch this person walk away into the distance and disappear over the horizon.

The easiest way to forgive someone, is to have compassion for them. I understand this is not always possible, as some people do commit heinous and unforgivable acts. But unless you're dealing with a monster, if you can recognise the other person's issues and insecurities, and understand how they were acting was due to their own weaknesses — then you can rise above your grievances and understand the situation from an empathic perspective. Empathy and compassion will neutralise negative sentiments.

It may also be appropriate for you to request forgiveness from other people for your actions. Maybe there are some ways in which you can redeem yourself and patch things up with people. Really make an effort to resolve, reconcile and let go of any negative entanglements you have with other people — then you'll feel much lighter.

If people make accusations against you and blame you, don't be defensive. Remain calm, admit any mistakes you perceive you've made and make a peace offering by proposing to make things right in any way that is appropriate. If they are not willing to accept your offer then it is best to walk away and not resort to confrontation. As long as you do not hold any grievances about what happened, you will remain unscathed from the encounter.

If a person is insisting you are wrong and is throwing all sorts of insults and projections at you. Seek to reconcile the situation as best you can, but even if you have made mistakes, you should remain self-assured.

You do this by assuring yourself you are committed to your development. And by remaining steadfast in this way, you can take criticism on board, you can learn from mistakes, and you can resolve ways to develop yourself. But if you enter into a frame of mind where you become deeply offended or hurt by other people's accusations and insults, you can end up internalising their projections. This can cause you damage, as you can start to believe their insults and adopt them as your own beliefs. Don't take criticism, rejection or insults over personally.

If you have to provide criticism to someone, remain calm, express yourself in a way that is honest and sincere. And try not to make the other person wrong. So, you don't become righteous, you simply explain the reasoning behind what you are saying, and if appropriate, you request that this person makes some changes. If you can avoid insults and demands then you will usually avoid unnecessary conflict and grievances.

It is quite common for people to criticise each other in ways intended to create guilt or shame. Again, be aware of your actions, take responsibility as appropriate, admit your wrongs, seek to resolve any issues and learn from the experience. If you follow these steps, then you need not succumb to any prolonged guilt or shame as a result of criticism.

People often gossip about each other and this can be very toxic. If you have any grievances that you cannot accept, then it is best to discuss these with the relevant people and to seek resolution. All too often, people will complain to everyone else in their life apart from the actual people they have the grievances with. This can lead to all sorts of issues as negative gossip breeds negative emotions and sentiments.

Seek to surround yourself with people who are balanced, cooperative and supportive. And don't get bogged down by negative emotions if you have to deal with people who behave in dishonourable ways. Life is too short. Control your reactions, and if you do have them, don't worry, just make an effort to let the emotions go as quickly as possible. This way, you'll avoid the ball and chain of grievance.

Responsibility

People often have rather elaborate tales about how they've ended up the person they are, and about how their life is as it is. Can you think of any stories you may tell yourself?

If any of your stories hinge on blaming other people and circumstances for your plight in life, then you have to accept what happened and take responsibility for what you can do now, in the present time. When you blame other people or circumstances, you are admitting to yourself that you don't have the personal power to accept or change the situation. You are reinforcing your sense of weakness. You are admitting that you are not willing to take responsibility.

When you accept responsibility for what happens in your life, you will have no one to blame, and that includes yourself. Blame requires an opposition, but when you take responsibility, you are able to accept yourself and your actions. You are able to learn from mistakes and persevere by making positive changes. You step beyond the inner conflict of self-blame by taking responsibility.

Be careful not to get stuck in a victim mindset as this attitude will reinforce a sense of insecurity and hopelessness. We are all victims to one degree or another, we've all had bad experiences in life, but if you identify mainly with the struggles of your life, you can generate a false sense of victimhood. Many people who identify as a victim cling onto stories about their suffering and their misfortunes. They use their stories as excuses for not doing certain things in life, and as a way of garnering attention. Victims crave sympathy for their struggles, and so they will often carry on generating dramas and phony impressions, in order to receive attention and affection.

There are many variations of victimhood. There are those who want attention due to their great sacrifices in life. There are those who want attention due to their weaknesses. There are those who think they deserve attention due to their specialness. And there are those who garner attention by purposefully being difficult and antagonistic.

So, the person who works hard at a job they dislike may play victim by making a big deal out of the sacrifice they are making to earn a living. A person who focuses too much on their failures and weaknesses, may play on the sympathy of others in order to get them to do things for them. A person who thinks they are entitled to certain things in life will play on their specialness and will expect others to provide for them. A person who doesn't appreciate what they do in life may make other people's lives difficult in a ploy to sabotage them, and lead them to feel a similar sense of hopelessness.

Everything can become a struggle to the victim, and they will often feel persecuted and can feel like the world is somehow against them. Yet, usually it is actually the opposite, as it is they, themselves, that are the obstacle to their own progress.

If you have any of these tendencies, you have to recognise when you are being disingenuous. You have to assess the beliefs you have about yourself rationally and push through anything that is phony or irrelevant. So, you look to see if you are acting in certain ways subversively. Are you acting in subversive ways because you want attention, status or to be rescued? Are you acting in subversive ways because you have certain expectations or crave certain desires?

What is the motive for your behaviour? Look to identify why you want to provide certain impressions to yourself and others. Look at why you make a big show about certain predicaments. Why are you motivated to generate these perceptions? Are you being sincere? Or are you scheming and being manipulative? Do you have a hidden agenda?

It usually all boils down to insecurities of some sort. And in order to rectify their insecurities, people learn ways to get their needs met. But if you have to be disingenuous or manipulative to get your needs met, this leads you down a shadow path. A path where you will not feel empowered by your own inner strength as you will be living under the shadow of your pretences.

This path can become rather perilous, as to maintain victim status, people will often go to increasing lengths.

Their incessant focus on their struggles can lead them towards increasingly self-destructive behaviours such as over-working, addiction or self-sabotage. All in an effort to maintain their victim status that they present to the world in a bid to receive more attention.

You avoid this path by taking personal responsibility. You live in a way that does not require people to perceive you in a certain light. You live in a way where you do not have to feign goodness, specialness, suffering or importance. In a way where you let go of any sense of entitlement, and you lower your expectations and desires of other people so that you are respectful of them. No more phoniness, no more bitterness, no more laziness, no more manipulation, no more excuses.

Once you don't have any hidden agendas underlying your actions, you can take responsibility for your life. And you can request what you want in an authentic way. So, if you want attention, you ask for it. If you need assistance, you ask for it. If you want achievements, you work diligently. You identify your needs and you become honest about them with yourself and others. You accept where you find yourself and you focus on your strengths and resources. You reinforce your sense of worthiness by taking actions that make you feel in control and that boost your self-esteem.

See if you can trace back any stories you have about yourself and your life. Question their validity. Are they rational? Are they still relevant? Then consider writing yourself a different story, one that is more accepting of yourself and your life. A story with compassion for your journey, that is also filled with hope for your future. A story where you take responsibility for your life.

Relating to Yourself

At first, it can be difficult to perceive some of your shadow traits and you will have to monitor yourself and spend some time in introspection. But once you start to notice them, you can begin to consciously recognise the inner friction that occurs if you feel like you are doing something wrong. So, you begin to notice the aspects of yourself that make you feel uncomfortable and dishonourable. You are no longer denying, ignoring or unconsciously acting upon your shadow traits — you have brought them into the light.

You must have great compassion for yourself during this process. And you must remember that many traits you may feel uncomfortable about, are not inherently wrong. For the most part, you were probably just acting from your desires and insecurities in an attempt to better yourself and your life.

So, you have to go beyond any shame you may feel. This shame may have been gnawing at you unconsciously for a long time, and if you become aware of shadow traits, it is important that you do not fall into consciously reinforcing shame. If you can recognise shadow traits and not depreciate yourself about them, then you can go beyond the negativity and make positive changes. You can learn about yourself and address any relevant insecurities wrapped up with the shadow traits.

Take notice of how you relate to yourself. How do you react to the things you do? The relationship you have with yourself is the key to going beyond any shadow traits. You integrate your shadow traits by accepting them and understanding the motives behind them. And you go beyond them by focusing on changing your attitudes, inner sentiments and behaviours as appropriate. You neutralise inner friction by becoming more authentic, compassionate and honourable.

You also have to recognise if you're feeling uncomfortable about your instinctual drives. Societal norms, values and religious concepts have conditioned people to feel a lot of guilt and shame about their thoughts, emotions and behaviours. And our personal expectations and desires can become supplanted by certain ideals, that can lead to the suppression of certain aspects of ourselves.

For example, you may feel guilty about being attracted to a person. But what is it that you relate to as being deviant? Perhaps you are already in a relationship or perhaps the person you are attracted to is in a relationship. But instead of feeling awkward about your attraction, why not simply appreciate the wonder of beauty and be grateful for the beauty of this person? You can't walk through a field of flowers and only notice one flower as being beautiful. Being attracted to beauty is natural, it is not a sin. It comes down to being genuine and honourable. So, you don't berate yourself and try to repress your natural attraction, but also, you are honourable in your actions. In this example, if you do not engage in infidelity, nor get carried away with lustful desires, then you shouldn't feel any guilt about the attraction you feel.

Sometimes, a person will end up committing acts they feel are dishonourable and disrespectful. But these people are usually not evil or committing any kind of crime. It's just that their desires or insecurities caused them to instinctively act in certain ways. And they did not have the discipline to restrain themselves, and perhaps the spontaneity of the situation swept them along so fast they didn't actually fully stop to consider the implications of what they were doing. For example, perhaps their attraction to another person resulted in them being unfaithful.

But it's often not as simple as judging these types of actions to be entirely wrong. It comes down to weighing up the choices you make in life and then dealing with how you relate to yourself and others about these choices. Sometimes, instincts and desires are very strong, but you can live to regret what happened. But sometimes the instincts and desires lead you to positive experiences you don't regret. Either way, if you end up feeling uncomfortable about what you've done, then you have to reconcile the situation and resolve the negative emotions as best you can, in order to forgive and make peace with yourself and others.

Processing your shadow is the process of accepting your natural instincts, whilst also adhering to a code of honour. It's a balance. So, it's not about repressing your feelings, it's about being disciplined and controlling yourself. It's about developing an empathic attitude whereby you respect other people, and you appreciate the needs of other people. You then recognise how to behave with honour. And therefore, if you decide you do want to pursue your desires, you pave a way for you to do so, whereby you are honourable and respectful to others. This way, you can avoid generating any inner friction about feeling uncomfortable about your actions. So, for example, a person would break off their current relationship before entering a new relationship. They honour their initial agreement to be faithful.

It is prudent to understand that there are ethical and moral standards that most of us do feel naturally primed to adhere to. So, it is wise to make an effort to be kind, respectful and honourable to other people. As the old adage goes, "Treat people as you would want to be treated." And to really internalise this fully, you have to expand the compassion you have outwards, and open your heart to the wider community.

Magnanimity

As you develop yourself and process your shadow, you will become more attuned to the needs of others. You can observe people from a place of non-judgement, and you can naturally develop an empathy that allows you to understand people.

You can understand why people act in certain ways due to their insecurities. And this understanding allows you to feel compassion for them. It doesn't necessarily mean you forgive them or agree with them — but it means you can liberate yourself of disgruntlement about their actions.

Once you realise the futility of resentment, disdain, blame, indignation and manipulation, you can then walk through life free from unnecessary emotional reactions and negative thoughts about others. You can transcend your own shadow traits and become authentic, compassionate and honourable.

You can communicate with honesty and offer no false impressions. You can respect people and be tolerant of their differences. You can adhere to a discipline of living by ethical principles. You can become genuine in your goodness. You can go beyond lip service and social niceties, and communicate and interact with warmth and compassion.

When you ask someone how they are, do you actually sincerely care how this person is? Try it next time you are in a shop, ask the person serving you, how they are, but really deeply mean it. Look them in the eyes and open your heart to this person.

When you hold a door open for someone, are you doing it just because it is the socially accepted thing to do? Or do you genuinely care about making this person's life a tiny bit easier for a moment? Can you act with goodness from a place of genuine care and compassion, and not simply because of social etiquette?

Can you go out of your way to help someone without feeling indignant? Without feeling like they owe you? Without feeling resentment towards them? Will you go the extra mile to serve someone if they ask for your help? Or will you begrudgingly do the bare minimum?

If you lend your friend some money, will you belittle them with sarcasm and condescension? Or will you encourage them or simply stay neutral?

If you are cooking for your friends, will you naturally give them the better portions? If you are on a busy tube will you graciously give up your seat for someone? Can you be genuinely generous?

Can you accept people for who they are without judging them? Can you allow them to do what they're doing without trying to control them?

Can you trust people without doubting them or suspecting them? Can you allow yourself to feel vulnerable and not worry about the outcome? Can you accept your fears and move forward with courage anyway?

Can you perceive situations from other people's perspectives? Can you be empathic and understanding about the circumstances of their life?

Can you treat complete strangers with respect? Can you tolerate those who do not share your beliefs? Can you be impeccably honest and sincere? Can you be patient with people? Can you respectfully hold your ground and not be swayed by the negativity of others?

Can you be truly grateful for all that you have? Can you be genuinely happy for people who have things that you would like?

Can you be equitable and fair in all your relationships?

Can you remain humble if you hold power over others? Can you remain honourable if you hold influence over others?

Can you walk through life, without any desire for recognition or acclaim, and simply act with integrity, and naturally spread goodness in this world?

CHAPTER EIGHTEEN

Developing Inner Power

Acceptance

- Accept that life has ups and downs and that this is normal. Don't take things personally. Lower your expectations of yourself at times. Diffuse any angst about your life by being grateful for what you do have. Accept any inadequacies you think you have, and do not disempower yourself through self-depreciation.

- Appreciate the journey and don't become obsessed with the destination. Don't fall into the trap of, "Once I get there I'll be happy." Let go of any negative yearnings that may be wrapped up with your desires. When you trust in your power to make changes to your life, you will develop a faith that allows you to more deeply appreciate all the interesting experiences along the way.

- Some emotional turbulence in life is inevitable. Don't deny your emotions. Allow them, admit them, face them and feel them through. This way you can avert any inner conflict that could be caused by trying to suppress them. Accept how you feel and accept what has happened in the past. Don't get stuck in self-generating cycles of emotions. Make strategic changes that will enhance your life and reduce stress and negative emotions.

- Acknowledge any disappointment you feel about yourself with self-compassion. Hold yourself accountable when appropriate. Learn from what happened, and commit to changes and resolutions that will prevent similar events from happening.

- Remember, ultimately you are the source of your own emotions. Do not disempower yourself by having unnecessary negative emotional reactions to circumstances that are out of your control.

- If you feel weak, then people will often take advantage of you. If you feel insecure, then people will often be afraid of you. When you are comfortable with yourself, other people will feel comfortable around you. A natural confidence within you builds as you feel more and more comfortable with yourself and what you are doing in life. Be genuine and authentic. Be you.

Respect

- Be respectful, kind and generous. Accept that people have different opinions and viewpoints and be open to discussion. But don't get caught up in emotional entanglements by trying to convince people your opinion is better. Always remain open minded and willing to change your views.

- Be inquiring, inquisitive and interested in people. Always remember you can learn something through every person you meet and every relationship you have. Allow people room to change and don't hold onto preconceived opinions about them.

- Give people support and encouragement when appropriate, but don't allow them to become overly dependent on you. Don't be afraid to say no if someone is taking advantage of you. By helping people to help themselves — you empower them.

- Communicate your needs to people in an honourable way. Negotiate compromises within your relationships as appropriate, whilst respecting other people's needs and values.

- Be aware of compassion fatigue. Don't give too much of your energy to people; whereby it becomes a detriment to your own health and well-being. Look after yourself and recognise your limits. Do not overly sacrifice yourself for others. Find a balance. Always remember to care for and respect yourself.

- Do not engage in gossip that is slanderous or unnecessary, it will drag you down and is not helpful to anyone.

- Try not to react with hostility to a person's behaviour as this can lead to feelings of insecurity. Without being defensive, communicate in an assertive and calm way when necessary. Describe what happened and how it made you feel, with no expectations or demands about a resolution, and with no intention to hurt or disparage. If you can do this without escalating into heightened emotions then reconciliation can usually be found quite quickly. Express how you feel, but don't play victim and accuse people of making you feel a certain way. Maybe the other person was in the wrong, but you should still take responsibility for your emotions.

- Do not allow people to dominate and unduly control you. Do not ever be unduly submissive to anyone. Don't get dragged into control dramas, disputes and conflicts. State your truth as appropriate and if an amicable resolution is not forthcoming then walk away. Make requests to people and always explain the rationale behind your request. Do not make demands. If you try and dominate and control people then you are insecure and afraid of them in some way, and they will not respect you. Insecurity can weaken your inner power, don't allow it.

- Let go of any resentment and anger you feel towards people, even if they have betrayed you and let you down. You deserve inner peace and it is not worth dragging yourself down with negative thoughts and emotions — let it go. Be compassionate for other people's weaknesses as appropriate. You don't necessarily need to forgive them, just disconnect from any negative thoughts and emotions regarding them. You can then release yourself from any friction that may have been weighing you down. Respect yourself by being at peace as much as possible.

Fortitude and Determination

- Take responsibility for the happenings in your life. If you get upset by something, always look for the silver lining. What can I learn? How can I grow from this? What can I do to make things better? How can I do better next time? Finding the silver lining is often the key to passing through emotional turmoil.

- Challenge any limiting beliefs you have about yourself. Ensure you address these beliefs by either letting them go or committing to making improvements. Focus on supportive self-appraisal and when appropriate set yourself challenges with the intention of changing an attitude or self-belief. To change an attitude or self-belief, you have to change any accompanying behaviour. You do this by taking action that counters the attitude or self-belief. So, you provide evidence to yourself that you are changing.

- Recognise how you interpret your circumstances and your performance. Understand how the power of your thoughts can affect you negatively. If necessary, challenge and change your interpretations. Don't jump to irrational or overly negative conclusions about your abilities or circumstances. Don't beat yourself up or be too hard on yourself. If you put yourself down, you'll go down, as will your sense of power and self-control. Remember, we are all here learning by experience as we develop and evolve. No one is perfect.

- Become self-assured about your own worthiness, your strengths and competencies. Maintain your integrity through your own inner validation. Do not rely on feedback and validation from others for your self-assuredness. Resist social pressure and conformity. Go your own way in life as much as possible within reason.

- Whatever happens to you in life, you have to recognise the responsibility you have. If you perceive events as mere chance and luck, you are not acknowledging the control you have over your life and you limit yourself. When you take responsibility, you take control of your life and you recognise the force within you to create potential, and through this recognition, you open yourself to receive.

- If something is bothering you, do not simply be passive and allow it to bother you, either accept it, or take some action to resolve it. Rationally assess situations, gather information and make decisions to take actions that lead to solutions. Remember, stressful and challenging situations are often the situations we can grow and develop from the most. The more you prove to yourself that you are capable, the more confidence you will feel. Then you will become more resilient. You will understand how to adapt and manoeuvre yourself appropriately. You will increasingly know what to do in any given situation.

- Learn about yourself and recognise the meaning in the things you do in life. The more meaning you perceive, the more you will appreciate your life. Act with purpose. Act in ways that are in accordance with your deepest values. You will then empower yourself with a deeper sense of meaning and purpose.

- Become the sole proprietor of your thoughts and feelings. Become your own task master.

- Think of life as a series of interesting experiences that you can learn from. Be prepared and willing to 'fail', and understand that life is a process of learning and developing. Remember, there is a lesson to be learnt in every situation you find yourself in.

- Don't blame other people or circumstances. Move beyond any notions of entitlement you may have. We are all victims in some regard, but don't fall into the abyss of victimhood by identifying as a victim and wallowing in self-pity.

- It is fine to hold people in high-regard and aspire towards role models, but don't unduly compare yourself to others. Be happy for people who have something similar to what you want. Any jealousy and resentment are signals that you are turning your focus to what you lack, and this will disempower you and make you feel insecure.

- Do not give undue attention to what other people think of you, as if you do, you can end up contorting yourself and conforming to their expectations in order to please them and be accepted by them. You do not need to prove anything to others.
- Challenge yourself by sometimes going out of your comfort zone. Even if you don't at first succeed, your confidence and self-esteem will be boosted by the act of trying. Stay calm, be patient and persevering.
- Makes friends with uncertainty. When the unexpected happens, try to act with intrigue and see what you can learn and take from the experience.
- Define your moral principles and be true to them. Make a list of your principles and honour them. By being self-assured about what you will do or won't do in certain situations, you fortify your resolve. You become unshakable in your code of honour.
- The decisions to act in your life should come from, '*I choose to*' not '*I must*' and this way, you maintain freedom and are in control of your life.

Focus and Attention

- Do not limit your life with restrictive thinking. Focus on the positive changes you want in your life, rather than any negative expectations or worries. Begin to push through any difficulties and make positive changes to your life. As you do this, you will enter a state of inner power.
- Use your imagination to visualise positive change and success. Visualise what you want to do going well, and your steps toward your goals being achieved. Evoke your senses and emotions in the visualisation. Really experience

it in your imagination as best you can. You are using your mind as a simulator and parts of your brain cannot distinguish between imagination and real world. The brain looks for consistency and by visualising what you want to happen; when you actually do it, you harness the power of coherence and assist yourself.

- Don't allow your mind to drift into past regrets or future worries. Focus attention primarily on the present moment and do what you can. There are always uncertainties, but you have to develop a trust in your power to adapt. Be willing to be flexible and creative as you pursue your goals.

- Fully let go of any old ideas or aspirations that you do not want to pursue. Clear your mind of clutter and focus on what is most meaningful to you.

- Don't think too much about your expectations of life. Consolidate your force of will and keep going. One foot in front of the other, with an inner trust in your ability to go beyond any expectations you could think of.

- Don't hold too many opinions or beliefs about yourself. And the few beliefs you do hold about yourself, make them empowering. Don't make too many assessments about yourself and the situations in your life. You do not need to evaluate everything, you can simply observe much of what happens in life. Quieten your mind, and only react when necessary.

- When you determine what you want to do, hone your attention and intention on it. Employ all your relevant strengths and resources, and act with dedication and perseverance. There may be challenges, there may be delays, but nothing, absolutely nothing can stop you if you remain disciplined, focused and determined.

- When you decide to relax, relax. When you decide to work,

work. Whatever you are doing, do it whole heartedly.

• Reading stories or watching movies in which there are themes of deep personal transformation can be very inspiring and empowering.

Empowering Techniques

• Recognise the many skills and resources you have. Remind yourself often of all the challenges you have overcome in life, and all of your accomplishments. Give yourself credit for the things you have achieved and all the things you do. Even the important things you may overlook such as parenting, cleaning, cooking. Do not overlook the meaning and value of many of the things you do in life. Truly appreciate all the good that has come from your efforts and make a habit of valuing yourself. Boost your confidence by focusing on your strengths and building on your competencies. Believe in yourself.

• Identify and remind yourself of all the positive aspects in your life — the people, the experiences, the things you have. Focus on what is going well and approach life with this focus as a foundation. Once a day, briefly review what is going well and appreciate the positive feelings this review brings. This will give you more resilience to deal with any challenges.

• Create a collection of memorabilia, quotes, photos and sacred items that have meaning for you and fill you with inspiration and positive feelings. Whenever you feel you need a boost, prime yourself with positivity by looking through this collection and connecting with the feelings generated.

• Write down a list of all the activities and experiences

you've enjoyed in the past — the times when you've deeply relaxed, had fun, been creative, felt inspired, found courage or overcome obstacles. Then use this list to check whether you are currently engaging in similar activities and experiences in your life. If not, then make plans and go and do what you enjoy. By taking the time to do things that provide you with positive emotions, you will feel more in control, happier and empowered.

- Make a list with two columns — in one column write what empowers you and makes you feel good, and in the other column write what restricts you and makes you feel negative. Use this list to create an action plan by which you do more of what empowers you and less of what disempowers you.

- If you feel weak, then pull towards you the memory of a time when you were feeling strong. Close your eyes and remember, focus clearly on how you felt, and bring those feelings to yourself in the present moment.

- When you feel strong and composed, take a moment to reflect on your feelings, take snapshots and add them to your repertoire of power recall. You can associate words or affirmations with these power recall moments to empower them further and make the recall process faster.

- Be humble. Have little desire for acclaim, popularity or status. Don't boast or show off. If you need people to believe in you, you are signalling that you don't believe in yourself.

- Align yourself to what makes you feel vibrant, strong and free. Surround yourself with people that makes you feel vibrant, strong and free. Align to what empowers you.

- Empower yourself by taking actions and seeing them through to completion. Prove to yourself that there is meaning and purpose in what you do. Prove to yourself that you are capable and strong by completing what you set out to do. Apply your strengths, skills and resources to accomplishing your goals.

Organisation and Discipline

- Manage your time in a way so that you are organised and pro-active. Avoid distractions as best you can. Work on specific small steps towards your goals. Maintain self-discipline through consistency, dedication and perseverance.
- Ensure you make time for activities you enjoy. Spend quality time with your loved ones and good friends, and also ensure you get some private time and solitude when you feel like you need it.
- Look after your physical and mental health. Maintain self-control. Stay balanced for the most part. Practice relaxation techniques and meditation in order to maintain calmness and develop yourself.
- Declutter and organise your space. Your external world is often a reflection of your internal world. If your home is a mess, your mind will likely also be disorganised.
- It can be very empowering to feel unburdened by stuff that you have to worry about and maintain. Lighten the load. Become minimal and focus on what is important.
- Make sure the things in your life that you do require are functioning and efficient. Look after what you need and discard anything that is broken or redundant.
- Keep your finances in balance.
- Be self-reliant and autonomous as much as possible. When you have to depend on others, make wise choices and go for people who are trustworthy, punctual and efficient. Seek

assistance and collaboration with people who inspire you and challenge you in a positive way.

Consistency

- Maintain a consistent quality in your attitudes and sentiments.
- Maintain a coherence between your thoughts, speech, feelings and actions. Keep closing the gaps between them.
- Always communicate clearly and honestly with people. Talk with sincerity about what you want, what you think, and how you feel. This way, you can avoid creating confusion.
- Value yourself and charge people accordingly for your services or products. Always agree your fee upfront in a clear and defined way and it helps to be consistent, even if you are working with friends or family.
- Be prudent in making commitments. Assert yourself and say no or delegate tasks to others as appropriate. When you do make commitments, honour and fulfill them impeccably.
- Consider changing your image to empower yourself and to be consistent with changes you are making in your life. New clothes, new haircut, new jewellery — whatever you feel confident and vibrant wearing. Also, consider working on changing your body posture and facial expressions. Little things like standing up straighter and smiling more can often increase confidence. But don't be fake about it — maintain authenticity.

Decisiveness and Spontaneity

- Be willing to trust your feelings, your instincts and your intuition. Opportunities may arise and sometimes if you are not spontaneous and decisive you can miss them. Be prepared to jump and trust yourself. The quicker you make decisions, the less time you will be confused and the more confident you will become.

- If you are confused about what to do, commit to doing something or accept that you are unsure and don't act. If you don't act, limit the time you spend pondering the choice. I recommend to gather information about the choices, assess each choice rationally, and then sit back and don't think about it. Trust your feelings and your higher processing abilities will take care of the rest and will provide you with clarity.

- If you have to make a quick decision, then don't worry about things not working out as you hoped. Remember, you never know, as maybe the 'wrong' decision will actually lead you somewhere interesting.

- Instead of saying, "I must do this at some point" do it now or schedule in a time to do it. Don't leave tasks and obligations hanging in the midst. As much as possible, if you see something you need to do, do it right then. The more you put tasks off, the more they will build up as clutter in the back of your mind. Get things done, and you will free yourself from unnecessary mental clutter.

CHAPTER NINETEEN

Meditation

Meditation is a process by which a person transcends their thinking mind and enters into a deeper more profound state of awareness, insight and relaxation.

You do not need to be a holy person sat in a temple to access this state. You do not need to be Buddhist, Hindu or be involved with practicing any form of religion or spirituality to benefit from meditation. I have never been interested in the many complicated forms of meditation and will only describe here simple methods.

The benefits of meditation are widely accepted and have been proven by many studies. In brief, meditation can improve cognition, memory, concentration and creativity. It can promote resilience and relaxation, and greatly reduce stress and anxiety.

Meditation can allow a person to garner realisations, clarity and composure beyond what is normally accessible. More than anything else, it is a tool for self-development, and can help a person to develop a greater understanding about themselves and their world.

Meditation is the gateway to accessing the full resources of your consciousness, it can take you beyond the ego to a more advanced perspective and understanding. But you do have to make a commitment and maintain a dedication to experience this. You have to seek a neutrality and stillness in your mind, beyond intellectual expectations and yearnings.

Time and Place

Meditating in the same place and at the same time each day can enhance your progress. It can help carry your momentum and maintain the discipline. It can serve to develop a rhythm within your body-clock and mind. You will become more and more accustomed to entering into a meditative state at this same time and place. Many people say that first thing in the morning is the best time to meditate, but it doesn't really matter.

When I first got into meditation, I was somewhat hooked and would meditate two or even three times a day, sometimes for twenty minutes, sometimes for two hours. These days I meditate less. I recommend a practice of at least twenty minutes once a day, but you should endeavour to discover what works best for you.

Posture and Pose

I never much liked the 'Lotus pose' as it is known, which is the classic pose of sitting cross-legged on a cushion on the floor with your spine straight. I think this pose is only beneficial for advanced meditators and yogis. If you are new to meditation, either sit in a comfy chair where you have back and head support or lay down on your back. What can happen, even for advanced meditators, is that you can slip into sleep or very deep states of consciousness and your muscles will let go. Until you are familiar with this process, it is best to practice meditation in a position where your body is supported, so that you won't twinge your neck or fall off a stool if you suddenly go deep!

It is recommended to sit up straight in a comfy chair and so use some extra cushions as necessary. If laying down, lay on your back with your head and neck comfortably supported. In either position, do not cross your legs or arms and just rest your hands on your lap or by your sides. Ensure you are warm enough. Sometimes body temperature can drop slightly when entering deep states of relaxation, but also keep in mind that if you are too snug it can induce sleep. Experiment and see what works for you.

Setting

If you have a space you can dedicate solely to your meditation practice then you can make it a sacred space by placing certain items there. Perhaps, photos of certain people or spiritual symbols that have deep meaning to you.

You could burn some incense during your meditation. I have found sandalwood to be helpful at inducing a meditative state. Do try and find good quality incense sticks made of natural ingredients. You could also use aromatherapy oils such as lavender to assist the process. Some music that relaxes you can be very beneficial, and is also a good way of keeping track of time without setting an alarm. Keep the space clean, free of clutter, serene and sacred. The colours of gold, silver, purple or deep sapphire blue are most complimentary for a meditation space.

If you can't dedicate a space solely for meditation, you can do certain things and use certain things only during your meditation practice. For example, you could have a particular blanket that you put over you only when you meditate. You could light a particular candle that you only light when you meditate. You could play a certain music track only when you meditate. These sole purpose items contribute to an inner understanding, that your meditation is a sacred dedication.

I used to lay on my bed and meditate a lot and found that if I laid the opposite way around on the bed, I could go deeper into meditation, otherwise, I would often fall asleep! So, if you're using your bed perhaps you could try this.

Opening and Closing

You can prepare yourself for meditation by using relaxation techniques such as the ones I have provided in the chapter Relaxation Techniques. All of these techniques can be very helpful for meditation and, in many ways, the visualisation methods are meditations.

A slow and deep breathing rhythm is highly beneficial for most forms of meditation. Gradually allow yourself to breathe slower and deeper as you begin to relax more and more.

Setting an intention or saying a certain affirmation when you open and close your meditation can serve to deepen reverence for your practice. You could also say a short prayer of gratitude or just be thankful and think of what you are grateful for. Perhaps consider chanting a mantra before you meditate. Maybe ring a bell or bang a drum to open and close. Or light a candle to begin and blow it out when you finish. Any action to delineate this sacred time you are making for yourself can be helpful to deepen the process and provide a greater sense of meaning.

External Tools

Some people like to use a prayer bead necklace which they hold and move the beads slowly between the tips of their fingers whilst meditating. This type of action can help distract and quieten the mind by focusing it on a mundane task. When the mind is occupied, a deeper state of awareness can then be accessed. It is a bit like when you're driving on a road you've driven on many times and you slip off into a daydream, and a few minutes later you think, hang on, who has been driving the car for the last few minutes?!

Shamans often use a drum or a rattle and will go into deep trance meditations whilst producing a repetitive rhythm. The key is to allow yourself to become attuned to the rhythm, and you can then end up sinking into the slower brain wave states known as theta or delta.

Crystal bowls can induce meditative states and are often used by sound healers. But it is difficult to keep the sound going by yourself during a meditation.

There are audio tracks that are composed of music specifically designed to induce meditative states of consciousness. I have provided a link in the Notes section at the back of this book.

It is also worth noting here, that practices such as Chi Gong and yoga are in many ways a meditation practice.

Some people are more suited to this type of meditation. Tension is released from the body and the movement can also feel very grounding. Both these practices always finish a session with a period of stationary meditation, usually laying down.

Internal Tools

Some people like to meditate on a particular image, such as a symbol, mandala or an image of a deity. They will focus on this image and visualise it during their meditation.

Some people like to focus on an affirmation, a mantra or a prayer during meditation. You can either say the affirmation, mantra or prayer in your mind if anything disturbs your peace. Or you can repeat the words throughout the meditation. Singing a mantra out loud throughout a meditation can be very effective for entering into a deep state of consciousness, but this will perhaps be quite distracting if you are new to meditation.

Others choose to focus on a particular feeling or topic. This can be as simple as focusing on the rhythm of your breathing. Or you can focus on an intention or a subject that you would like information and understanding about.

The key, is to focus on the image, affirmation, mantra, feeling or topic — but not to think about it. Just repeat the words or hold the topic of focus at the background of your mind.

Inner Worlds

Many people imagine and visualise themselves being in a special place during a meditation. This is usually a relaxing and peaceful place in nature, however, some people enjoy visualising being active, such as rowing a canoe across a lake or hiking up a mountain. They will often create an inner journey for themselves where there is a starting point and an end point.

The inner worlds you create are limitless and as you become more adept at visualising, you can explore further and further into your imagination. As you go deeper in your inner journeys, you may even find yourself walking through doorways into inner worlds that are not scripted by your imagination. If this happens, then allow yourself to explore these inner realms. If you feel uncomfortable at all, remember you can always rotate yourself out. So, you simply turn and move in a different direction. There are no rules, so you can spin around, do a back flip or simply fly off somewhere else if you want. You can also choose to maintain an anchor point in a sacred and safe inner world that you can always quickly return to should you want to. You can associate a word with this sacred place, so when you say the word, it will pull you there.

To fully relax and go on an inner world journey in meditation, it is sometimes easier to have someone else guide it for you, and paint the imagery for you. There are many good quality guided meditation audios that you can find online.

Non-Object Orientated

This is when you simply go into meditation and you observe whatever comes. So, for this method you would not use any tools or visualisations.

I mostly use this method, and the reason is due to my experiences with Ayahuasca. Ayahuasca is an entheogenic plant medicine brewed by shamans in South America. During my work at shamanic retreat centres in Peru, I drank Ayahuasca on many occasions. The experience takes you into profoundly deep states of consciousness.

In the early days, I would go into Ayahuasca ceremonies with specific intentions and questions I wanted answering, only to find again and again that my intentions were irrelevant to my experience and my questions were not answered. Gradually, a level of inner trust developed and I realised that there is an inner wisdom — an inner guidance system that is based in subtle feelings, beyond the normal thinking level of the mind. Once I began to trust this and detach from my thought processes, my journeys on Ayahuasca, and also my meditations, became much more fruitful.

The process of surrendering is the key, and you do that by allowing yourself to become completely neutral. And the only way to become neutral, is to relax and maintain an inner poise of non-reaction. No thoughts, no emotions, no judgements, no opinions. Once you attain this state, you can drift into the void of inner peace where an ineffable stillness is experienced.

When you get proficient at reaching this state of inner peace, then you can enter into a subtle dialogue with your consciousness. It can become more like a shamanic vision quest than a traditional meditation. Solutions can appear, premonitions, information about how to help people, inner knowings... many things.

The main purpose of this book is to guide the reader towards this inner peace. And usually there is some physical and mental baggage that has to be resolved, before being able to arrive. This was certainly the case for myself and also many of the people I have worked with. But rest assured, with a little dedication — anyone can arrive at inner peace.

Meditation Practice

Decide which elements to incorporate into your meditation practice, and remember it is perfectly fine to keep it very simple and minimal. Get comfortable, close your eyes, and slow and deepen your breathing gradually at your own pace. If you are tense, the Body Scan relaxation technique can be very helpful to do as a prelude to a meditation.

If you notice you are feeling any particular emotions, simply allow yourself to feel the emotions. Don't struggle against them, just focus on relaxing your body, and as you further relax, you will notice the emotions will begin to ease. You could choose to do the emotional processing technique I described in the Understanding Emotions chapter. Being in a relaxed state can be a very good time to work with this technique. Or you can simply bring your attention to what you are grateful for in your life and this will usually neutralise surface level emotions, and allow you to calm yourself and proceed with meditation.

Observe any thoughts that arise, but try not to think further about them — just observe them, but don't react to them. Allow them to drift in and out. You can think of your thoughts as clouds that come and go with the wind. Much of what will arise is the chatter within your mind about your concerns and commitments in life. It can be useful to realise what is on your mind and things that are floating around in the background can come to the surface. Observe what comes. But just keep allowing your mind to clear by not thinking or reacting. It can take some time to master non-reaction, as our minds are often used to bouncing from one thought to the next, but with practice, you will be able to meditate and simply observe. So, don't concern yourself with what can seem like distractions arising in your mind, it is all part of the process. Observe, but don't react.

As you progress with meditation, you will find yourself to be calmer and more organised in life. Your body becomes more relaxed and your mind becomes more coherent and composed. You will naturally find that you have a greater sense of clarity. You realise what is important more readily, and you realise what to let go of more readily. As your meditations become clearer and less cluttered by thoughts and emotions — your life becomes clearer and less cluttered by thoughts and emotions.

Beyond the initial stage of a regular meditation practice, you will begin to enter into a dialogue with your subconscious. Symbols, images, people's faces, places — all sorts of quick visions will pop up and some of it will make sense to you, but some of it will not. Partly, this is happening because you are entering into the dream state whilst still being awake. And just like when you are dreaming, what is often experienced in meditation is the unravelling of your subconscious processes. And in a similar way to dreaming, much of what you experience in meditation can also be shown in metaphorical and symbolic representations. Through this process, you can begin to become more aware of belief patterns and emotions that are affecting your life.

Another benefit of meditating, is more restorative sleep. This is because a certain amount of subconscious processing is achieved through meditation, meaning that you will not need to dream as much during sleep. Long term meditators often only need four or five hours of sleep.

As you continue your meditation practice, sporadic thoughts, emotions and imagery will crop up less and less. And you may then experience periods of deep stillness where nothing seems to be happening. If you experience this, simply enjoy the peace and trust the process. The more time spent experiencing this deep stillness, the more you will expand your inner journey.

Beyond this stage, you can begin to gain access to a more profound stream of information. Perhaps you will have certain feelings, insights, understandings and you may also see visions. Some of the information may be relevant to your life and some of it may be related to aspects beyond your own life.

You may start to access information that is gleaned from the subtle influences of the people you've been in contact with. You can begin to understand that thoughts and feelings exist also as energies, that are transmitted and can be received by consciousness. Your intuitive abilities will develop. And can go well beyond the occasions when you think of your friend five minutes before they phone you.

You do have to be somewhat discerning about information you receive in meditation. And it is best to review any information you receive after your meditation is finished. Otherwise, the flow of information within the meditation tends to get stifled or mixed up with your thought processes or imagination.

If you receive information about other people, it is usually best to be discreet, unless you really feel it is appropriate to tell them. Stay humble and grateful, and this will allow you to access a pure stream of information that is not contaminated by egocentric desires.

As you get more advanced, you can start to use your feelings to navigate in meditation. You can feel around a topic for solutions, you can explore into visions, into memories, into situations, people and places. You can receive information and understanding. But you have to remain emotionally detached and not allow your mind to drift into analysis. Many things can then be revealed, there really is no limit.

As you get more and more in touch with this advanced level of consciousness, you become attuned to an inner guidance system that helps you to better understand what to do in life. You develop an expanded form of perception that extends beyond, but also compliments, your normal cognition.

Your consciousness outside of meditation will then also experience a transformation, and you will be able to access this expanded perception in your normal waking state. At first, it may seem like an occasional overlap, but as you progress, this advanced state of consciousness you have nurtured in meditation, will then become freely available to you.

CHAPTER TWENTY

Living With Honour

When you honour yourself, you take care of yourself. You look after your body by nurturing it and maintaining it. You consume the right balance of nutrients you require and you do what you can to avoid excess exposure to toxicity. You move and exercise in the rhythm that your body needs to feel supple and agile. You drink plenty of clean water and you ensure you get sufficient time in nature and in the sun's light.

You also take care of your mind. You look after your mind by nurturing it with calmness and relaxation. You ensure that you sleep well and do not burden yourself with over-thinking and worrying. You expand the capabilities of your mind by stretching yourself with challenges and new experiences. You empower your mind through the practices of meditation and visualisation.

You honour yourself by accepting yourself and your life. You let go of past grievances and take responsibility for your life. You let go of yearnings and you feel contentment. You let go of any pretences and you become genuine. You let go of any self-depreciation and you focus on your strengths. You let go of your stories and you allow yourself to change. You let go of doubt and you believe in yourself. You let go of worrying and you trust yourself. You let go of pride and become humble.

You transcend your social conditioning and your cultural programming, and you step into your authenticity. You honour who you truly are and you make peace with yourself. You simplify your life, focus your attention on what you want, and you move towards it.

You honour the meaning and purpose that you perceive in your life, and you allow this to guide you. You become balanced and composed. With patience and perseverance, you take action to attain your goals and fulfill your potential. There are no more failures — only challenges that present opportunities to improve, adapt and go beyond.

When faced with challenges you remain resilient. Through your tenacity you generate strength, and through your humility you blossom with grace. You abandon struggle, refine your abilities and develop a fortitude within yourself that is unbreakable.

You honour yourself when you dedicate your life to your evolution. You live with honour when you realise that part of your evolution involves serving others.

You serve others by being authentic, compassionate and honourable. Your authenticity serves others when you are genuine, honest, sincere, self-assured, reasonable, straightforward and humble. Your compassion serves people when you are kind, gracious, magnanimous, forgiving, affectionate, empathic, accepting, allowing and generous. Your honour serves people when you are steadfast, resolute, loyal, punctual, committed, tolerant, reliable, trustworthy, ethical, respectful and equitable.

As you live by the codes of authenticity, compassion and honour, you develop a deep gratitude and reverence for the people in your life and for yourself. Your philosophy of life then begins to change and you realise that because you have honoured yourself; you now have the strength to truly honour others. Without any hidden motives for reward or acclaim, you seek meaning and purpose in your life that revolves around serving others and working with people on collaborative projects to bring about positive changes.

You feel strong and centred in your individuality, and the qualities you honour and value in yourself; you can share with others when you are asked to. You enter into a pure state of loving kindness — a grace by which the balance of acceptance and love you hold for yourself can be naturally shared with other people.

Your inner power becomes rooted in a deep gratitude and reverence. You don't take people or circumstances for granted. You sincerely take time to thank people and you make a conscious effort to be grateful for all the good in your life. You make a short gratitude statement or prayer each day whereby you give thanks for people, items and situations in your life — even the small things.

Reverence allows you to be resilient and persevering in life. You deeply appreciate and savour the meaning and purpose in your life. You focus on the positive feelings that you want to further experience, and you expand into them with reverence. The positivity you revere then becomes a part of you — you internalise what you revere — you become aligned with what you cherish. You develop the ability to absorb your experiences more deeply, and by cherishing, delighting and revering them, you can expand your feelings.

As you enter into a deeper appreciation of life, your perception expands into deeper levels of understanding. Your consciousness transcends, allowing you a more advanced perspective.

By making peace with yourself and by living with honour, the world around you becomes more peaceful and honourable. May it be so.

Adrian Connock

September 2021
Ireland

Notes

Chapter 1 — Health Basics:

- Food list with corresponding primary nutrient:	
Protein:	**Carbohydrates:**
amaranth	fruits
dairy products	grains, whole
eggs	legumes
fish	sugars
grains, whole	vegetables
legumes	
meats	
poultry	
quinoa	
beans	
lentils	
hemp	

Vitamin A:	**Vitamin B1:**
blueberries	eggs
chilli, red	fish
corn	grains, whole
dairy products	legumes
eggs	meat
fruits, yellow	blackstrap molasses
liver	nuts
prunes	organ meats
tomatoes	poultry
vegetables, dark green	yeast, nutritional
vegetables, yellow	
Vitamin B2:	**Niacin (B3):**
dairy products	dairy products
eggs	fish
fish	grains, whole
grains, whole	legumes
legumes	meat
meat	meats, organ
meats, organ	peanuts
blackstrap molasses	poultry
nuts	brewers yeast
vegetables, leafy green	
yeast, nutritional	
Vitamin B6:	**Vitamin B12:**
banana	dairy products
fish	eggs
grains, whole	fish
legumes	meat
meats	
meats, organ	

blackstrap molasses potatoes poultry vegetables, green leafy wheat germ brewers yeast	
Folic acid: asparagus avocado beans broccoli Brussels sprouts bulgur dairy products fruits, citrus whole grains liver meat meats, organ okra oyster raspberries salmon sunflower seeds vegetables, leafy green vegetables, root wheat germ whole wheat brewers yeast	**Pantothenic acid:** dairy products eggs fish fruits grains, whole legumes meat meats, organ nuts royal jelly salmon vegetables wheat germ yeast
Biotin: banana	**Choline:** cabbage

dairy products	cauliflower
eggs	eggs
fish, saltwater	fish
grains, whole	grains, whole
legumes	legumes
liver	meat
meat	meats, organ
mushrooms	oats
oats	soybeans
peanuts	vegetables
poultry	wheat germ
rice, brown	brewers yeast
soybeans	
yeast, brewers	
Inositol:	**PABA:**
beans	dairy products
cantaloupe	grains, whole
dairy products	meats
fruits, citrus	meats, organ
grains, whole	molasses
legumes	mushrooms
liver	poultry
meat	vegetables, green leafy
molasses	wheat germ
nuts	
oranges	
raisins	
whole wheat	
brewers yeast	
Vitamin C:	**Vitamin K:**
acerola berries	leafy green vegetables

beans, sprouted	eggs
berries	soybeans
broccoli	blackstrap molasses
Brussels sprouts	cauliflower
cantaloupe	broccoli
cauliflower	Brussels sprouts
currants	cabbage
fruits, citrus	liver
grains, sprouted	oats
guava	whole wheat
kale	rye
kiwi	dairy products
papaya	kelp
parsley	
peas, green	
peppers, red, green	
rose hips	
squash	
strawberry	
tomatoes	
vegetables, green leafy	

Vitamin D:	**Vitamin E:**
butter	avocado
cod-liver oil	eggs
eggs	grains, whole
fatty fish	legumes
meats, organ	meats, organ
sunlight	molasses
	nuts
	seeds
	vegetables, leafy green

Bioflavonoids:	Carotenoids:
citrus fruits	dark green vegetables
fruits	yellow/orange vegetables
black currants	tomatoes
buckwheat	watermelon
onions	guava
apples	apricots
black tea	peaches
soybeans	cantaloupe
blueberries	pumpkin
	pink grapefruit
	mango

Calcium:	Chromium:
dairy products	brewers yeast
green leafy vegetables	whole grains
dried figs	dairy products
tofu	meat
turnip greens	liver
kale	mushrooms
broccoli	beets
okra	grapes
soybeans	honey
beans	raisins
sesame seeds	clams
whole grains	black pepper
quinoa	
almonds	
Brazil nuts	
hazelnuts	
molasses	
amaranth	

Copper:	Manganese:
oysters	nuts
nuts	whole wheat
seafood	whole grains
legumes	leafy green vegetables
whole grains	pineapple
potatoes	blueberries
green vegetables	seeds
meat	legumes
organ meats	eggs
raisins	tea
almonds	avocado
blackstrap molasses	seaweed
Potassium:	**Iron:**
blackstrap molasses	oysters
fruits	meat
avocado	organ meats
banana	poultry
legumes	fish
green leafy vegetables	dried fruit
vegetables	blackstrap molasses
potatoes	apricots
tomatoes	raisins
dairy products	leafy green vegetables
whole grains	eggs
dried fruits	cherries
almonds	whole grains
peanuts	legumes
sunflower seeds	oysters
fish	dulse
meats	

poultry	
Magnesium:	**Selenium:**
nuts	Brazil nuts
whole grains	sesame seeds
beans	brewers yeast
dark green vegetables	whole grains
fish	tuna
meat	wheat germ
kiwi	fish
dairy products	herring
molasses	oysters
	clams
	organ meats
Sulphur:	**Vanadium:**
beans	corn
Brussels sprouts	dill
cabbage	fish
dairy products	meat
eggs	mushrooms
fish	olives
garlic	parsley
horseradish	radish
kale	soybeans
meats	whole grains
onions	
peppers, hot	
turnips	
wheat germ	
Iodine:	**Molybdenum:**
seafood	legumes
seaweed (kelp)	leafy green vegetables

	whole grains
	dairy products
	organ meats
Silicon:	**Omega-6 fatty acids:**
cucumbers	black currant oil
grains, whole	borage oil
vegetables, root	evening primrose oil
	grapeseed oil
	meats
	nuts
	peanut oil
	poultry
	seeds
	sesame oil
Zinc:	**Fats:**
brewers yeast	Saturated fatty acids
crab	animal fat
dulse	beef
eggs	butter
fish	coconut oil
herring	fatty meats
kelp	lamb
meat	pork
mushrooms	veal
organ meats	avocado
oysters	cashews
peas, black-eyed	macadamia nuts
pecans	olive oil
poultry	peanut oil
pumpkin seeds	peanuts
sardines	pistachios

sunflower seeds soybeans turkey wheat germ whole grains	pumpkin seeds walnut oil walnuts fish flaxseed oil flaxseeds grapeseed oil sunflower seeds sesame oil sesame seeds soybeans
Omega-3 fatty acids: chia seeds fish oils flaxseed oil flaxseeds greens, dark leafy hemp oil hemp seeds pumpkin seeds Purslane soybeans walnuts walnut oil roe mackerel anchovies herring salmon sardines whitefish	

tuna, albacore turbot shark bluefish bass, striped tuna lake trout Atlantic sturgeon	

- Information about Digestive Enzymes:

Website: www.draxe.com/nutrition/digestive-enzymes

- List of Alkalising Foods:	
Vegetables:	**Fruits:**
artichokes	avocado
cabbage	lemon
carrots	lime
radish	grapefruit
watercress	watermelon
spinach	pear
turnip	apple
garlic	banana
lettuce	berries
asparagus	cantaloupe melon
onion	grapes
peas	peach
leeks	kiwi
chives	
celery	

kale Brussel sprouts cucumber	
Seeds, nuts & legumes: pumpkin sesame flax sunflower almonds lentils	**Drinks:** water vegetable juice non-sweetened soy milk almond milk herbal teas
Fats & oils: olive flax evening primrose coconut	

- Gut Reset guidance:

Link: www.draxe.com/nutrition/detox-diet

Link: www.draxe.com/health/microbiome

Link: www.medicalnewstoday/articles/3-day-gut-reset

Chapter 2 — Bypassing Toxicity:

- Foods least and most contaminated by pesticides:

Link: www.eatingwell.com/article/15808/15-foods-you-dont-need-to-buy-organic

Link: www.eatingwell.com/article/15806/the-dirty-dozen-12-foods-you-should-buy-organic

Chapter 3 — Detox Methods:

- Detox Instructions:

Website: www.thedetoxdudes.com

Follow the links on the website to sign up for the Free Detox Manual. You will then receive a download link. Email promotions will follow, but you can easily unsubscribe. I have no affiliation and have not used the paid services offered. For more specific detox advice you should contact a medical or naturopathic professional.

- Liver Flush:

Book: The Amazing Liver Cleanse by Andreas Moritz

- Lemon Master Cleanse:

Website: www.themastercleanse.com

- Naturally detoxing and cleansing foods list:	
Ginger	Dandelions
Blueberries	Fennel
Beetroot	Turmeric
Broccoli	Sesame Seeds
Cauliflower	Wheatgrass
Cabbage	Hemp
Kale	Cold Pressed Olive Oil
Artichokes	Onions
Almonds	Pineapple
Brazil Nuts	Asparagus
Lemongrass	Basil
Coriander (Cilantro)	Avocados

Parsley	Lemons
Cinnamon	Watercress
Cranberries	Apples
Garlic	

Chapter 4 — Movement, Exercise & Bodywork:

- Basic Acupressure body points for stress relief:
Website: www.thechalkboardmag.com/acupressure-chart-stress-relief

- Basic Tapping Tutorial:
Website: www.thetappingsolution.com/tapping-101

Chapter 11 — Nutrition For Your Mind:

- Tryptophan containing foods:	
Chicken	Flax Seeds
Turkey	Sesame Seeds
Beef	Cashew Nuts
Pork	Pistachios
Tofu	Almonds
Beans	Oats
Lentils	Buckwheat
Shrimps	Roasted Soybeans
Salmon	Caviar
Sardines	Apples
Cod	Bananas

Eggs	Prunes
Pumpkin Seeds	Cheese
Sunflower Seeds	Chocolate
Chia Seeds	

Chapter 19 — Meditation:

Meditation assistance audios:

www.quietearth.org

- - -

Source materials and hundreds of further resources relevant to the subjects covered in this book are listed at my website:

www.adrianconnock.com/resources

- - -

This book is available in paperback and Kindle via all Amazon websites. It is also available as an ebook for Kobo and Nook devices. Reviews and ratings are welcomed.

www.adrianconnock.com/books

Printed in Great Britain
by Amazon

17012112R00149